Landscape Flowers

Adults Coloring Book

This book belong to

....

Color Testing Page

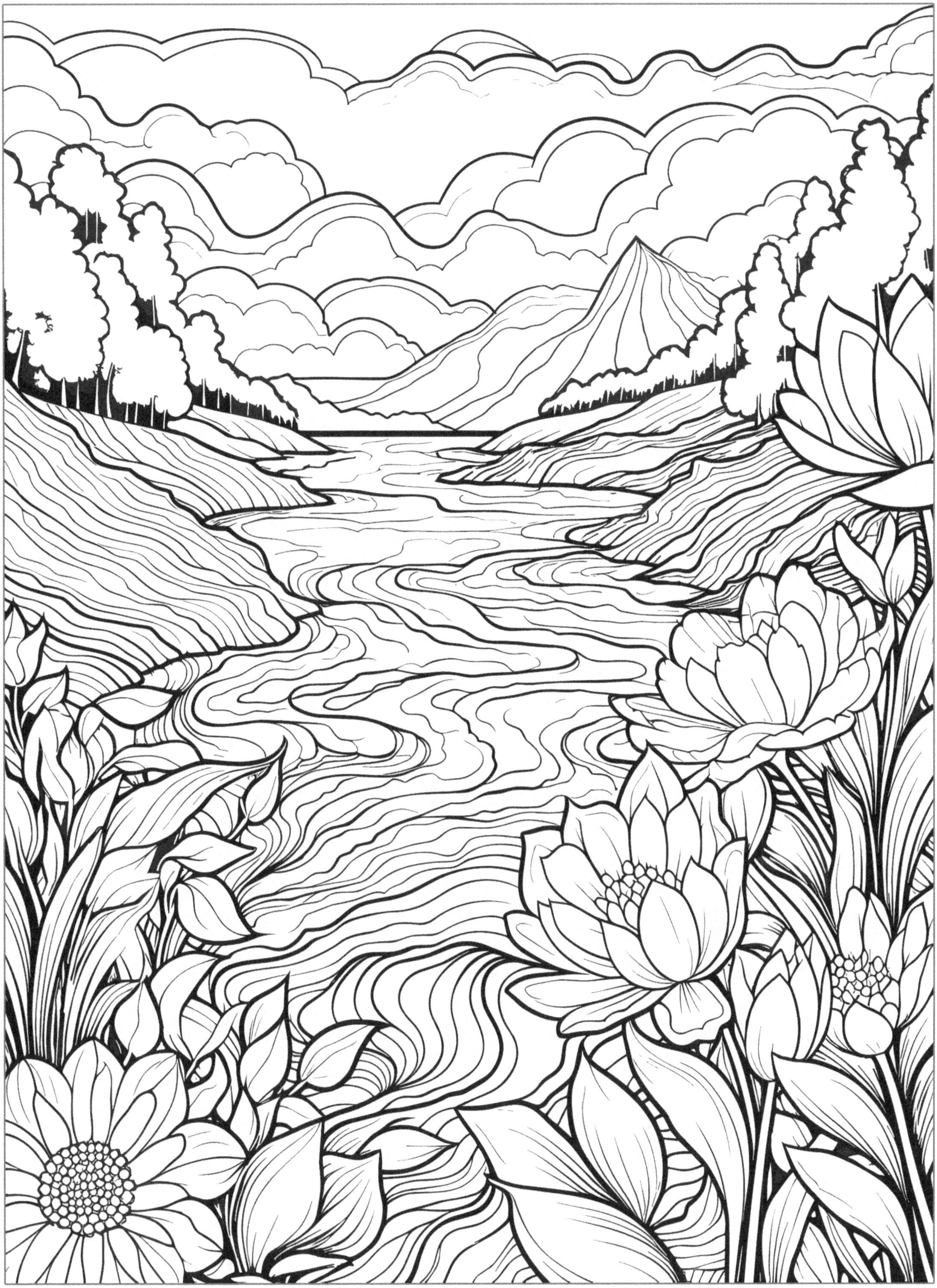

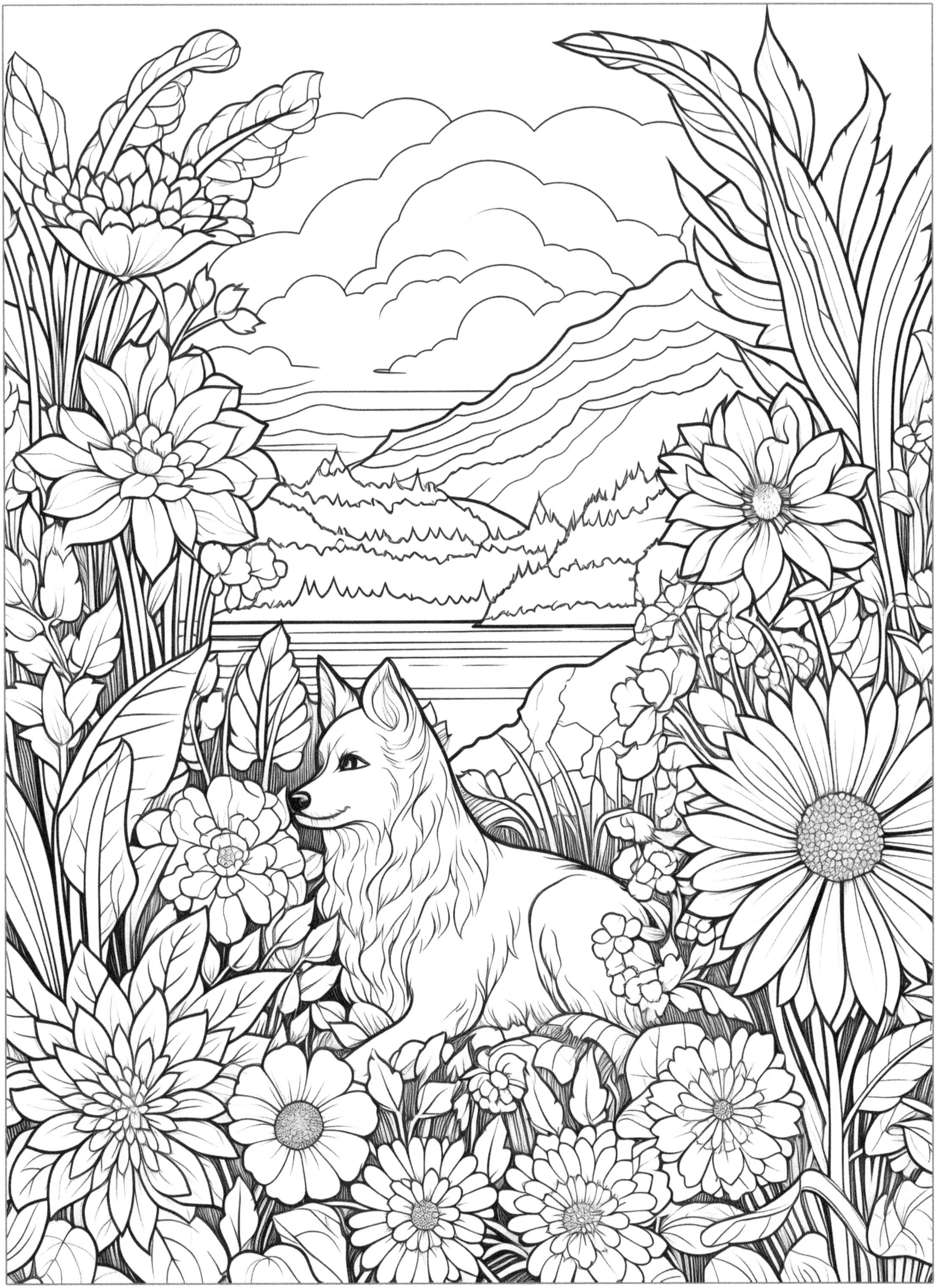

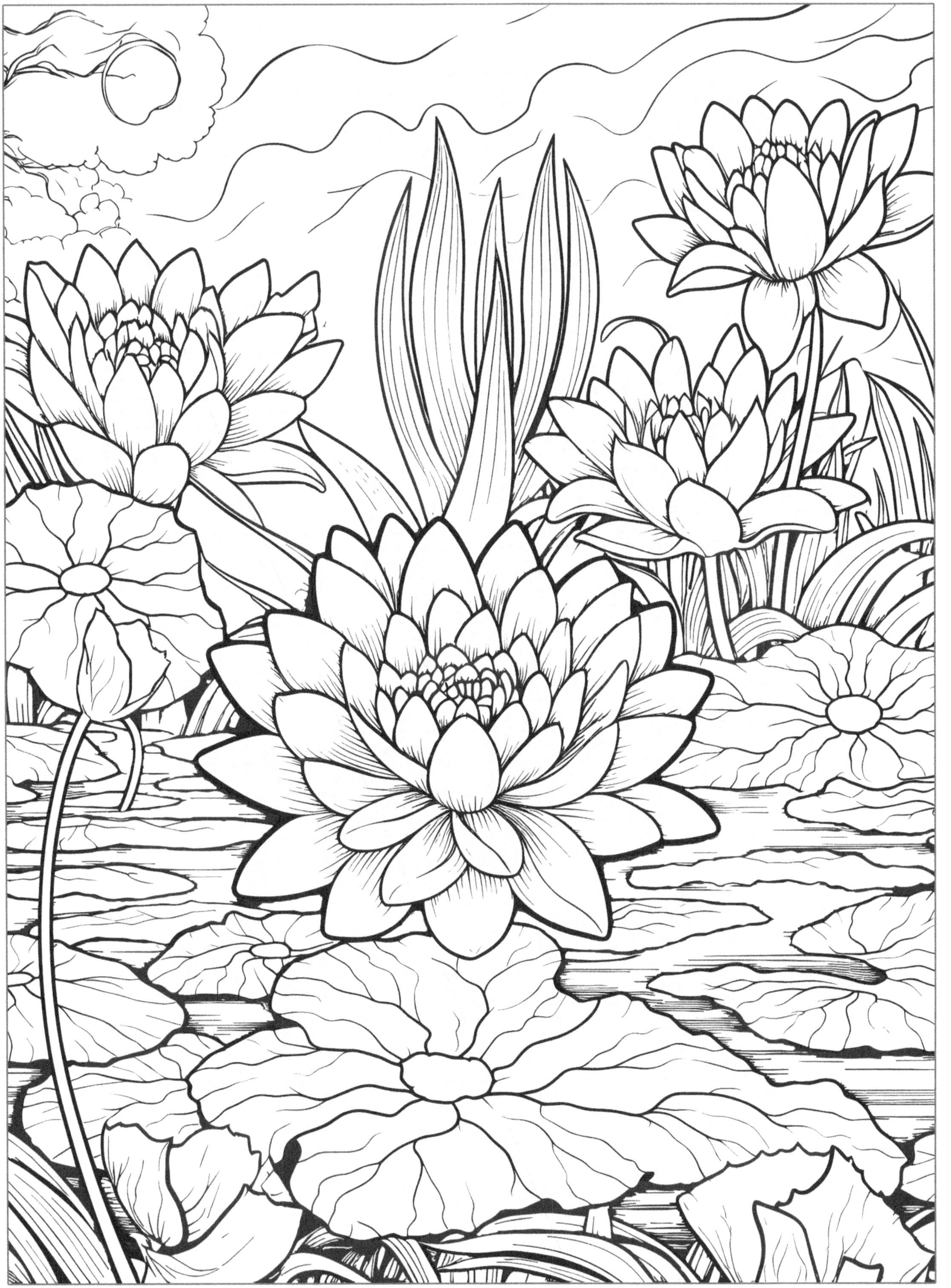

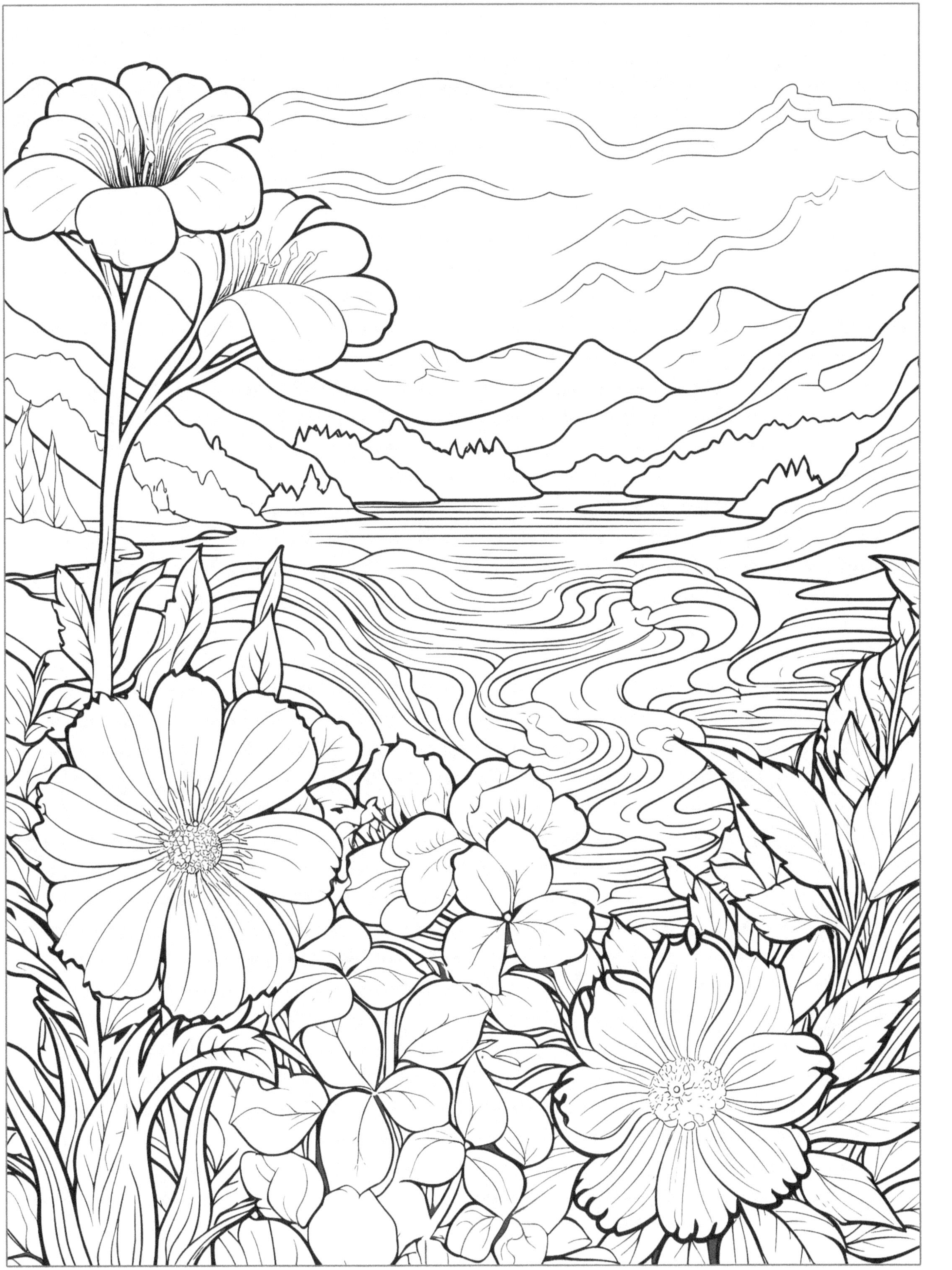

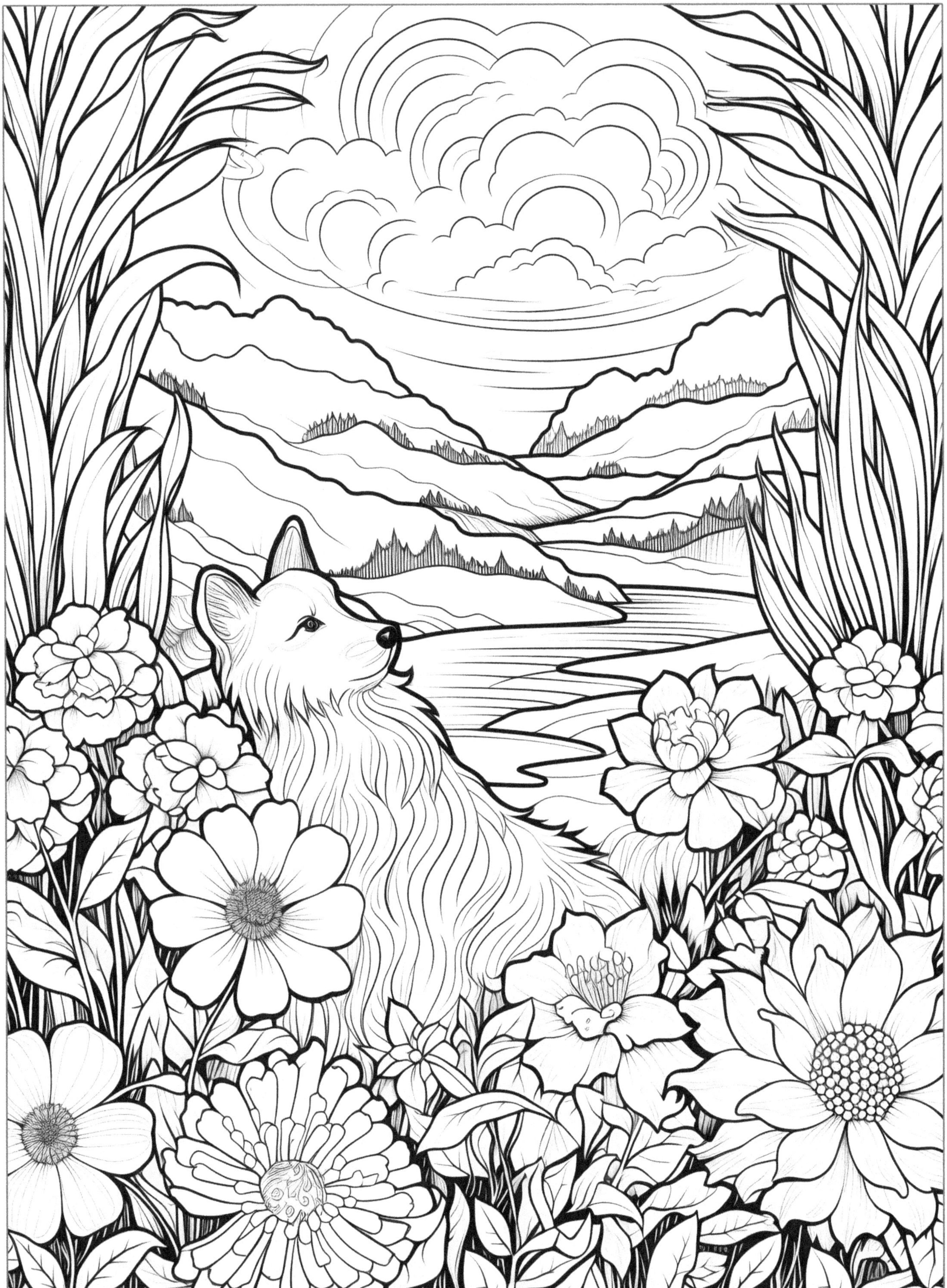

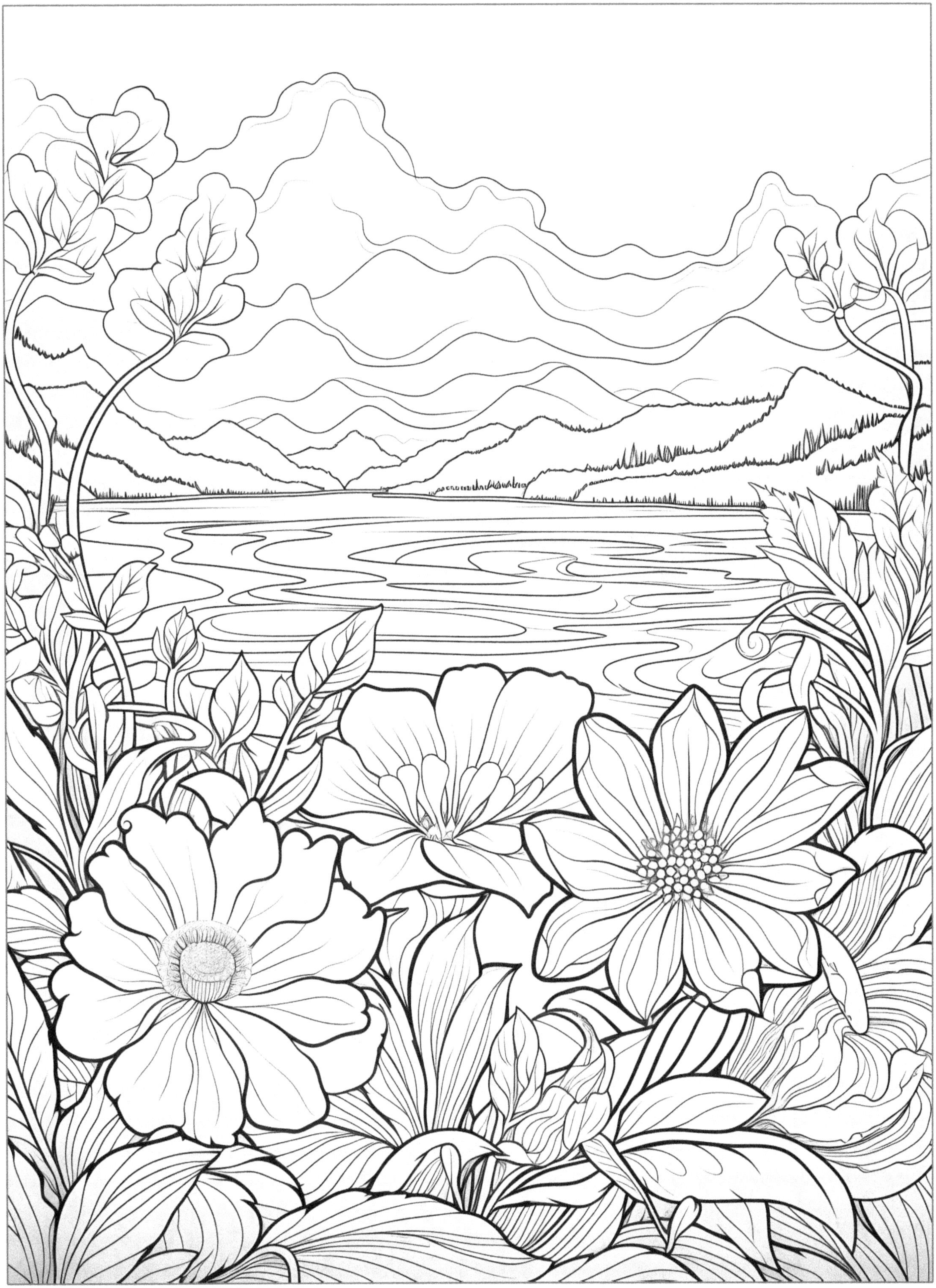

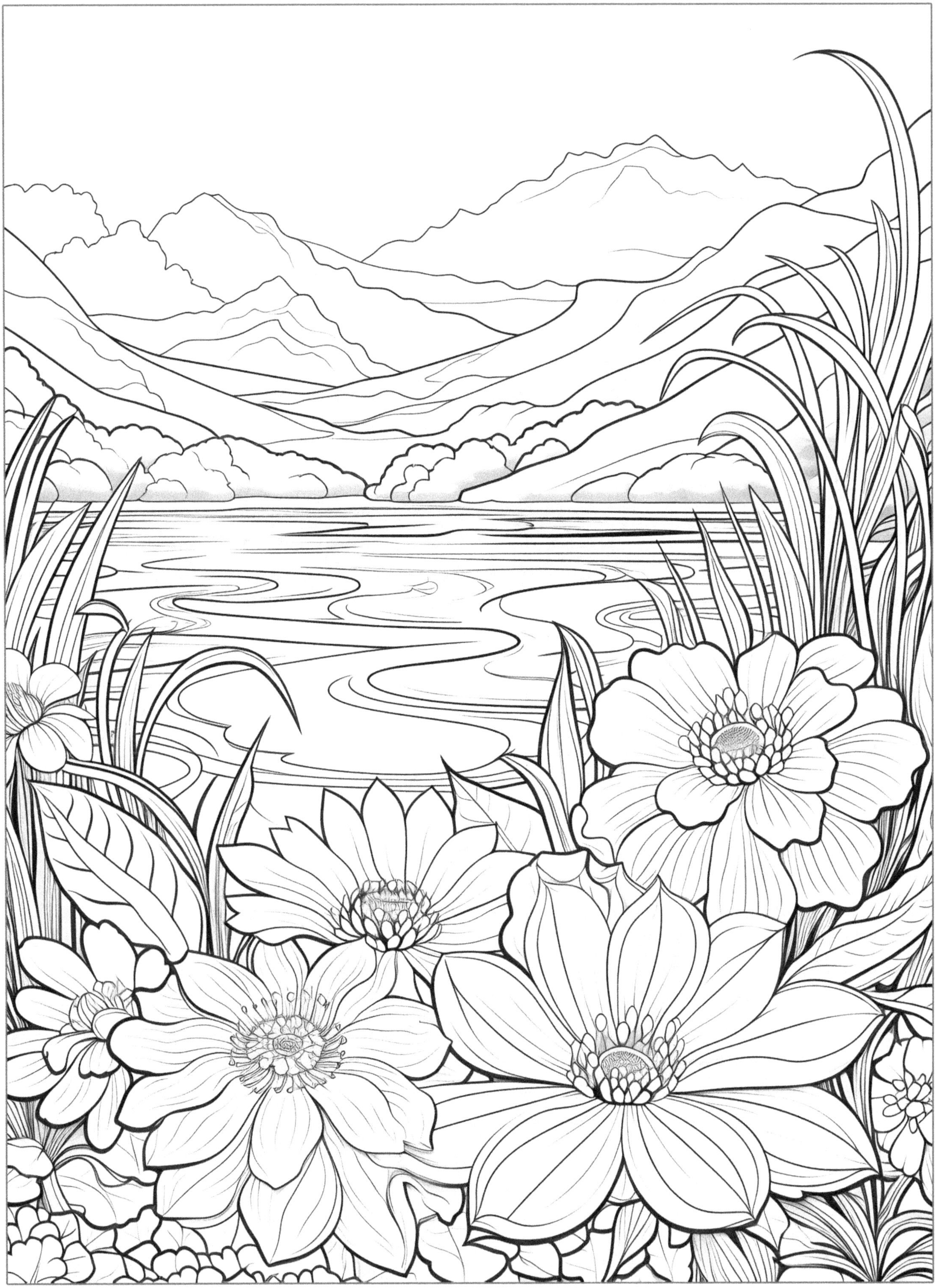

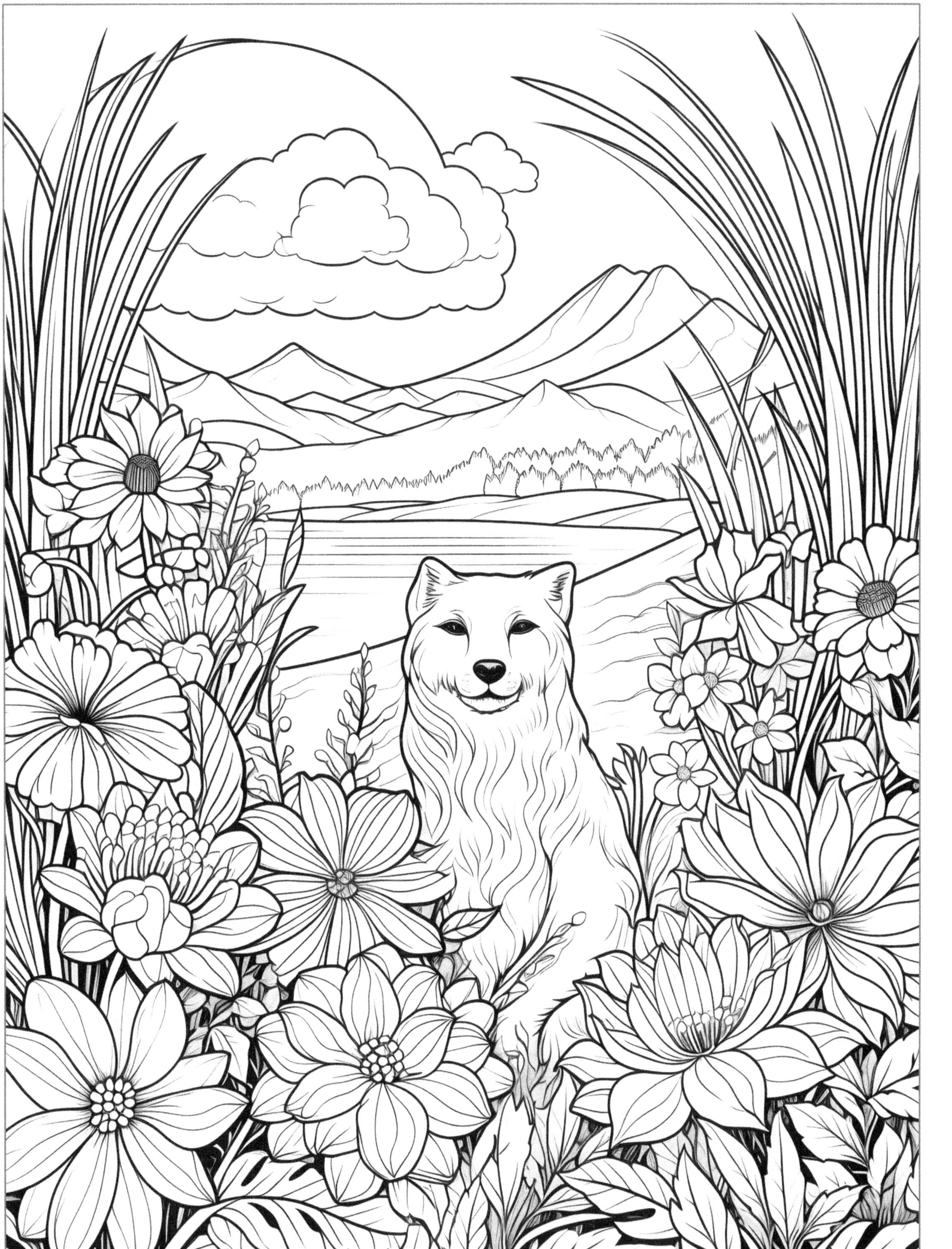

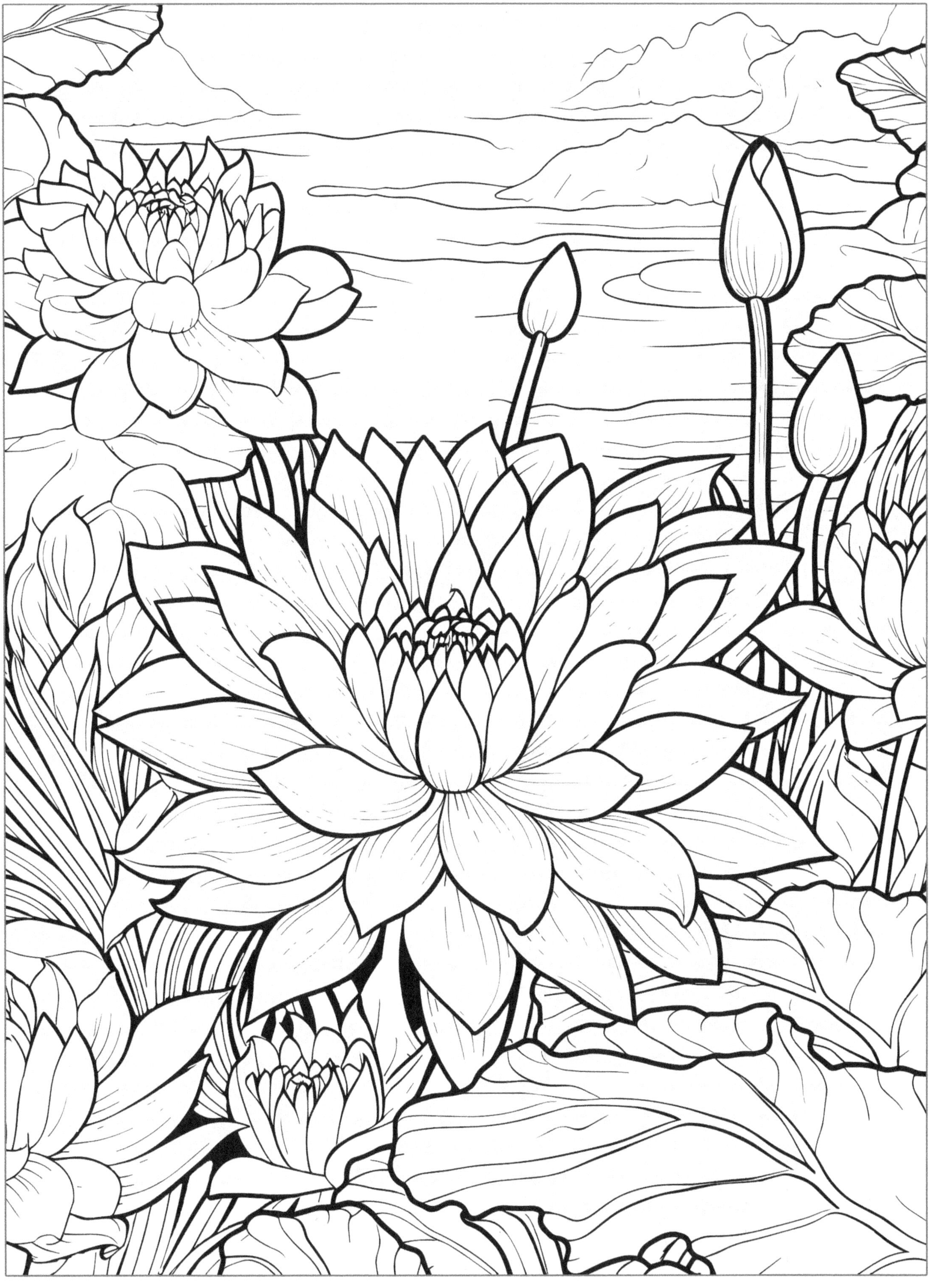

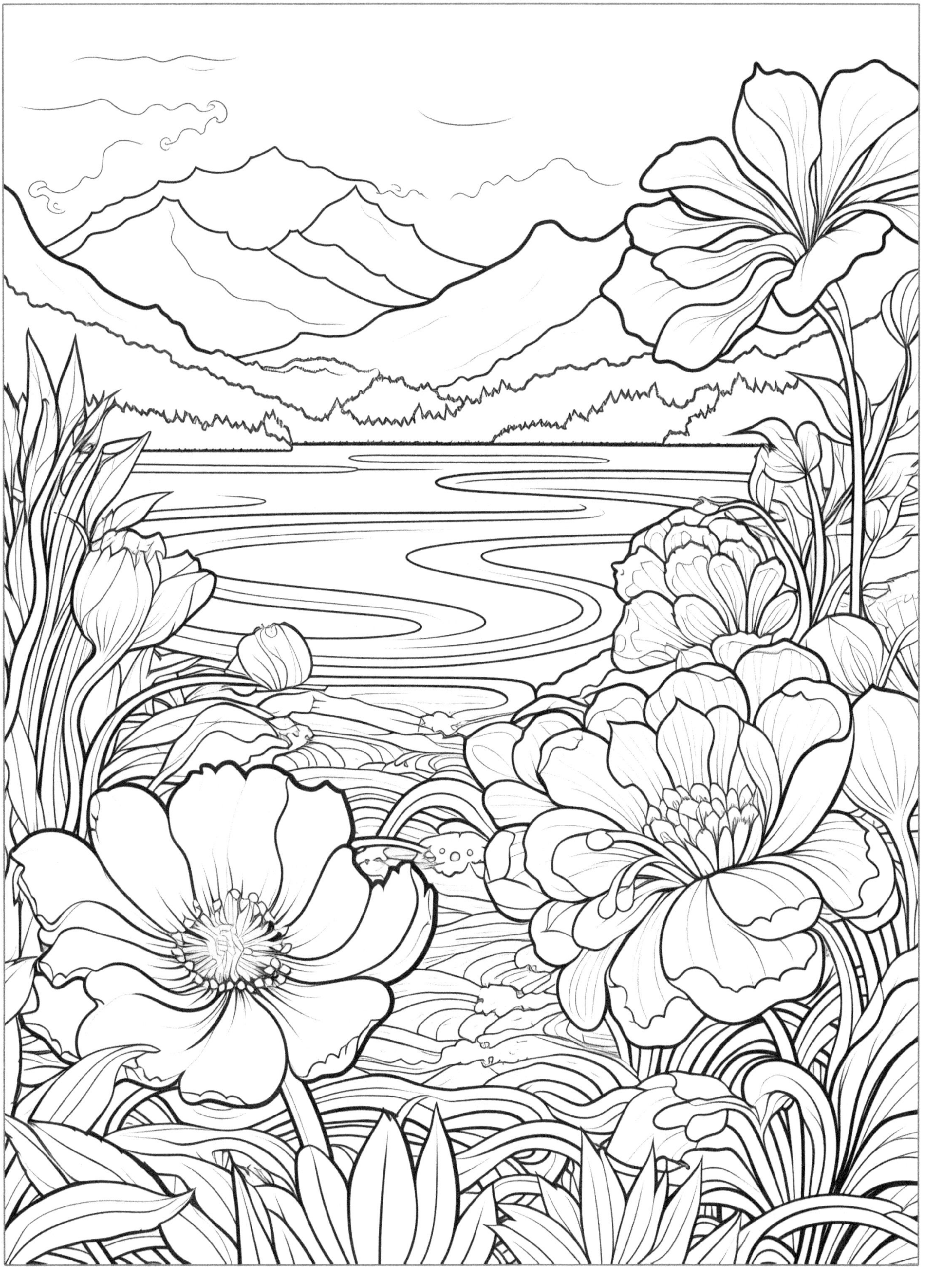

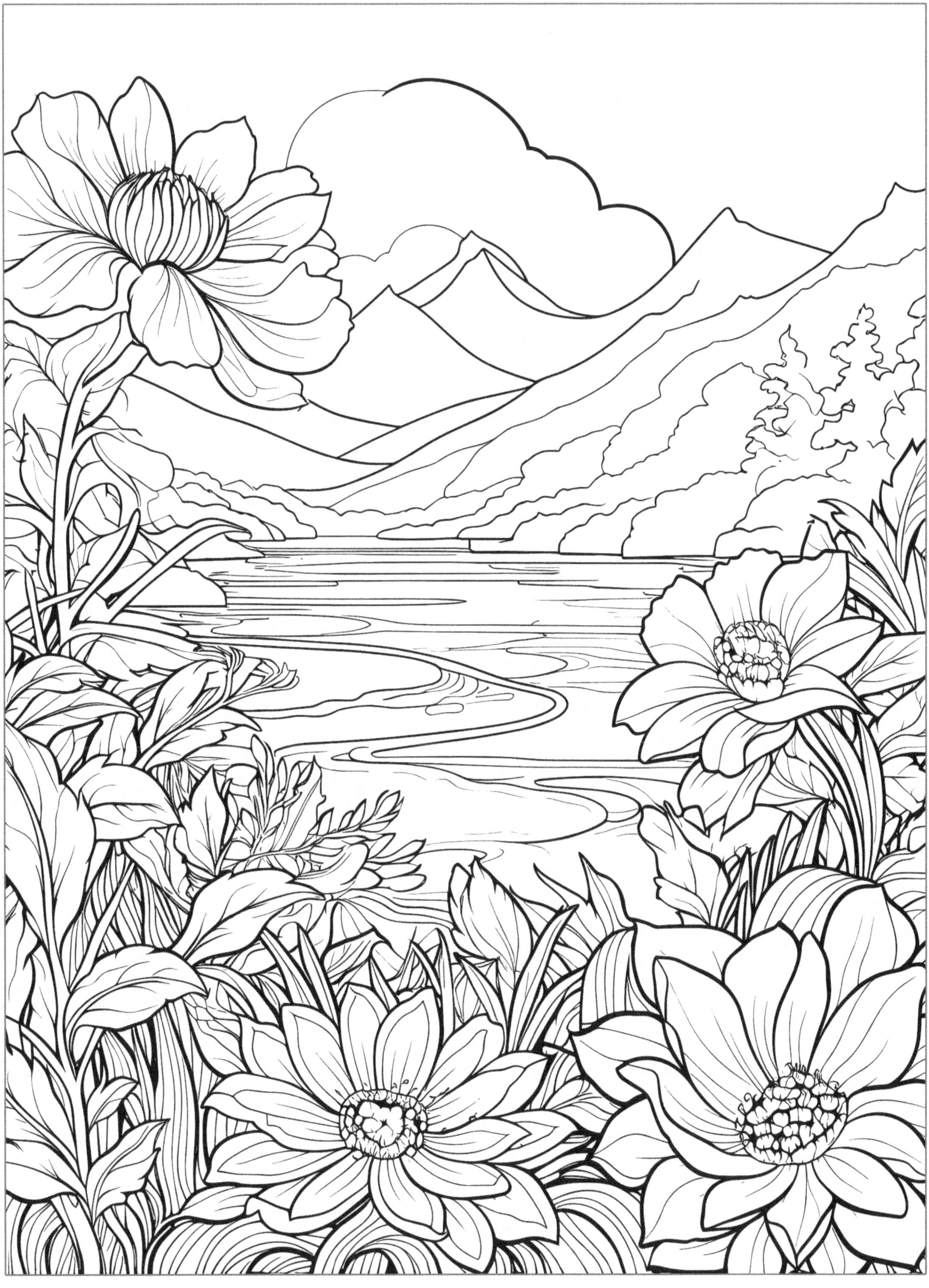

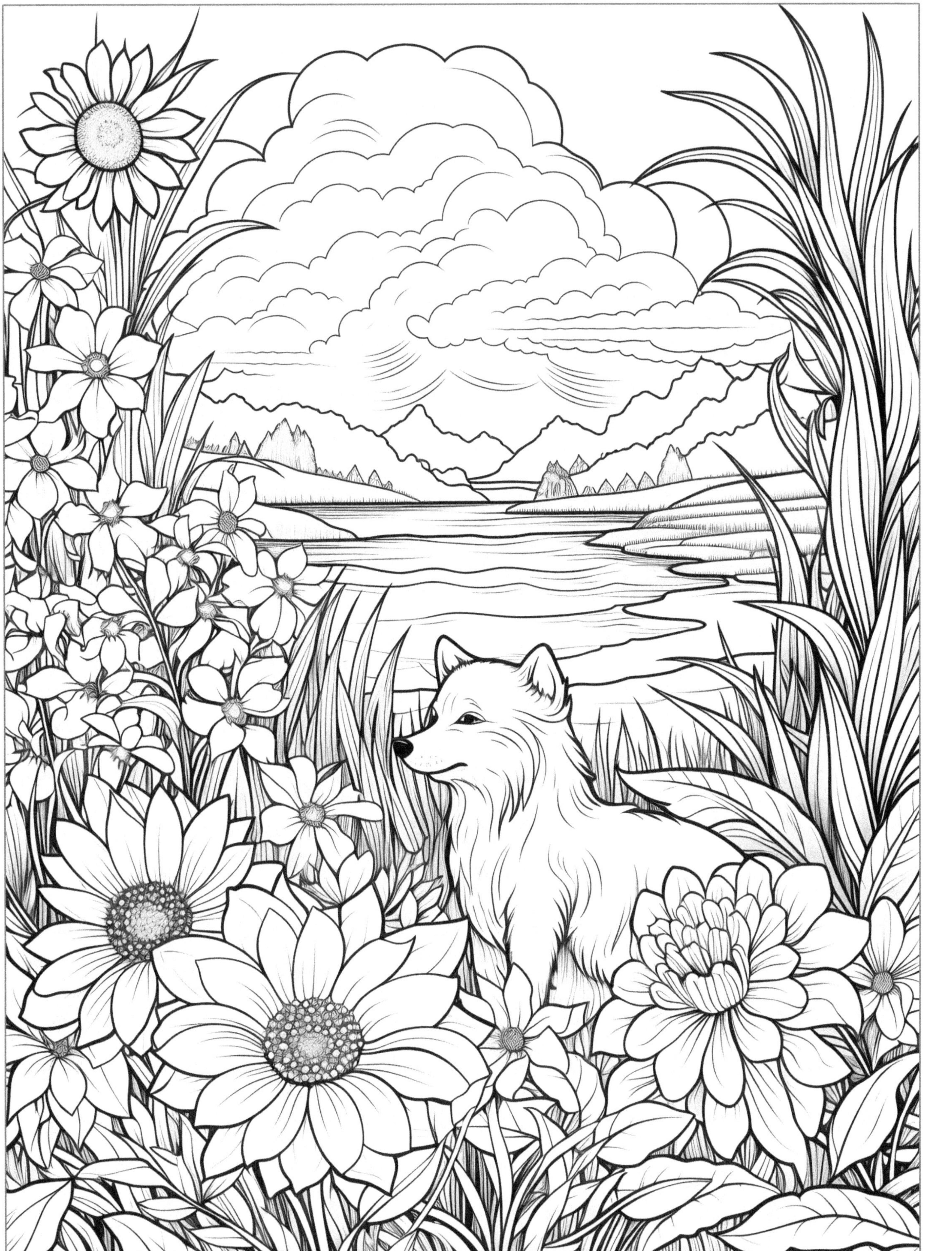

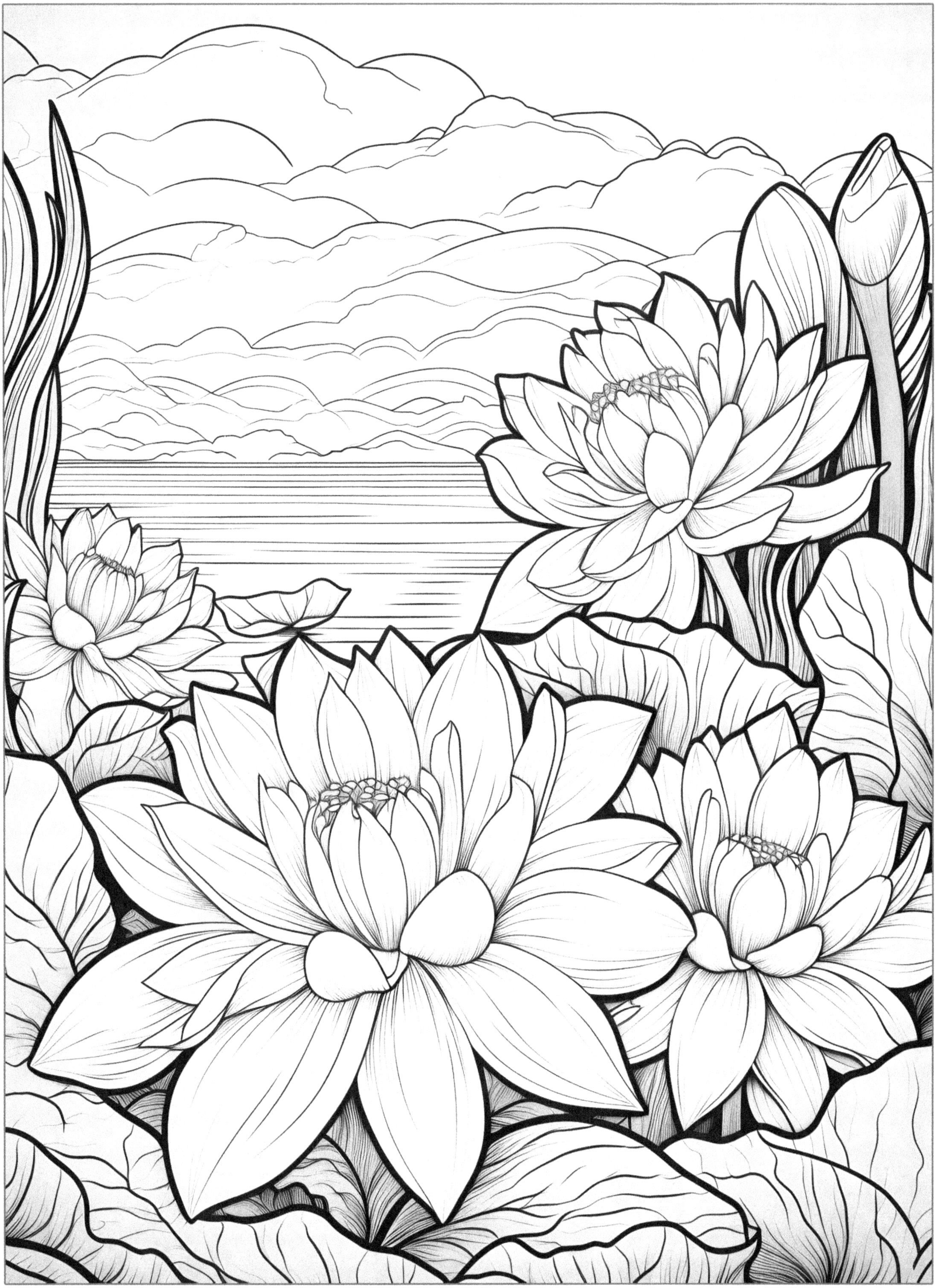

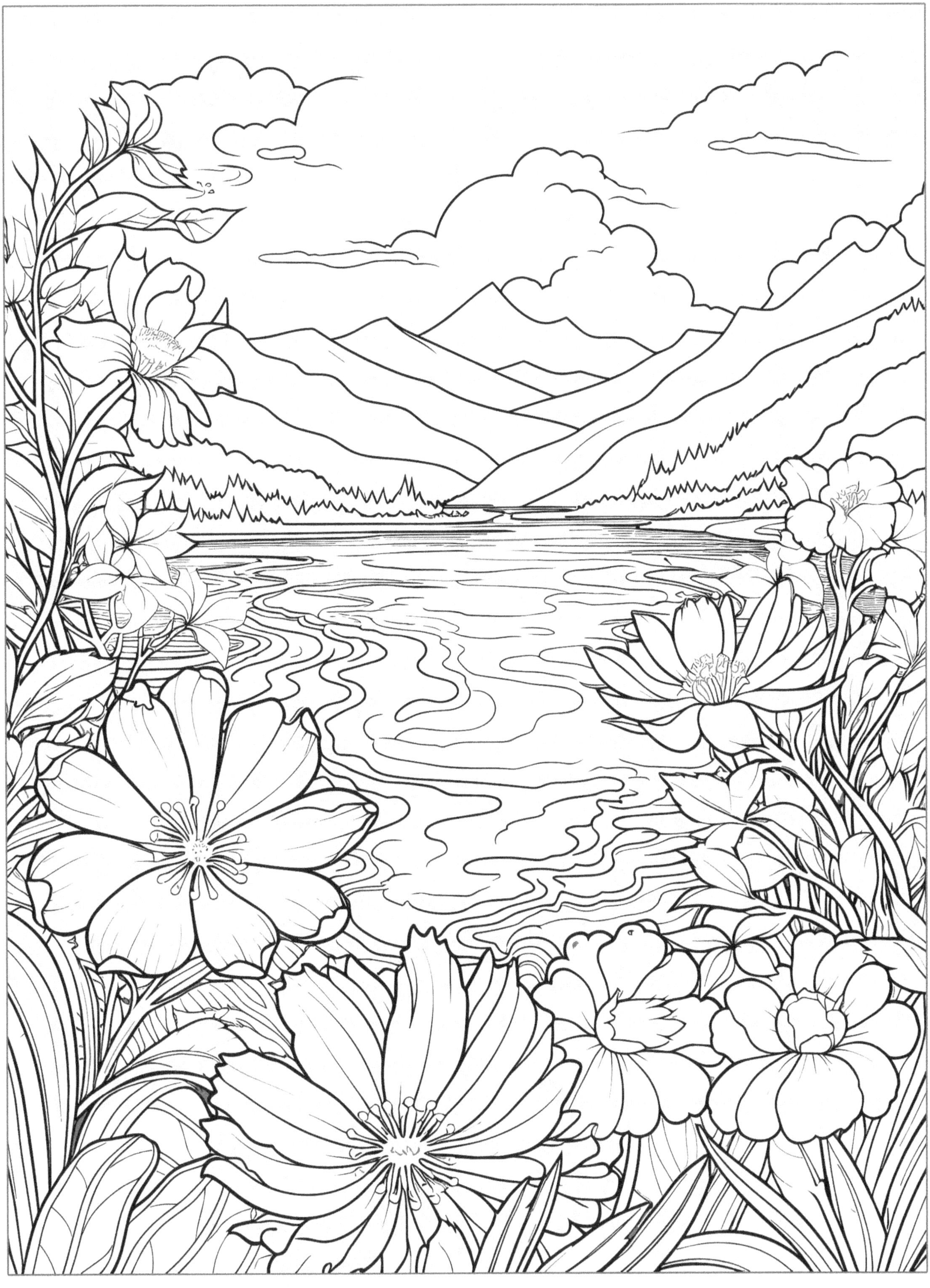

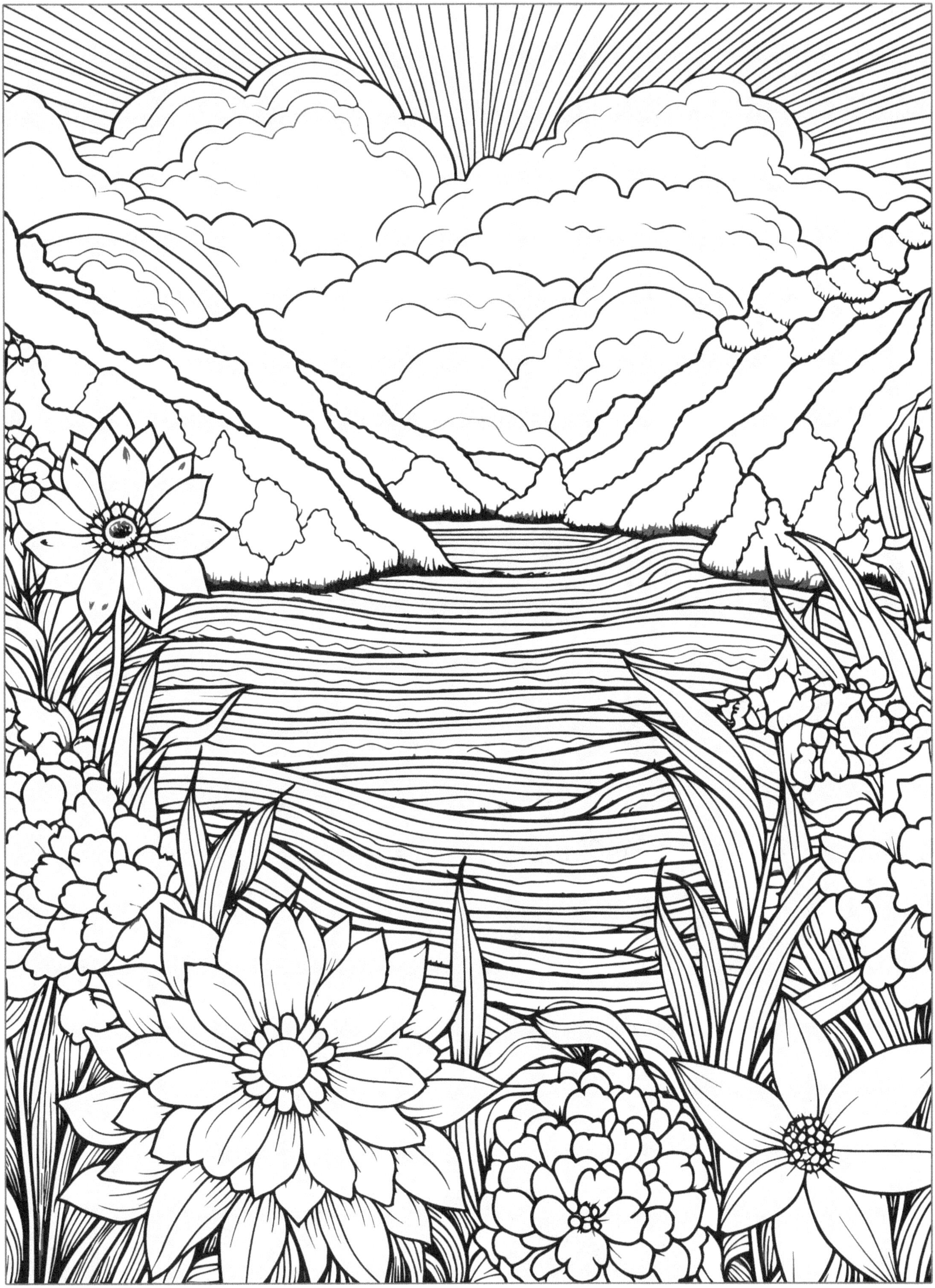

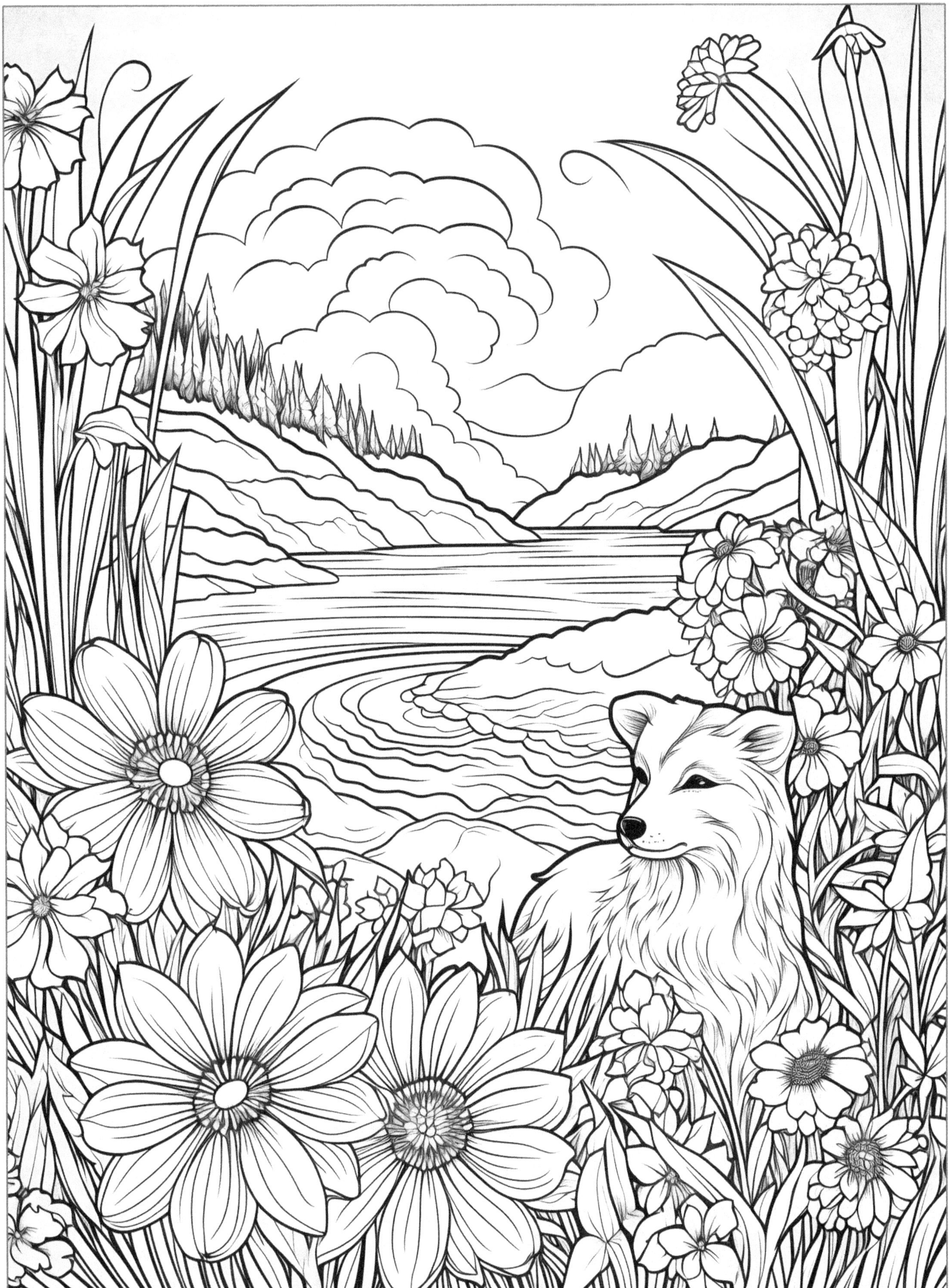

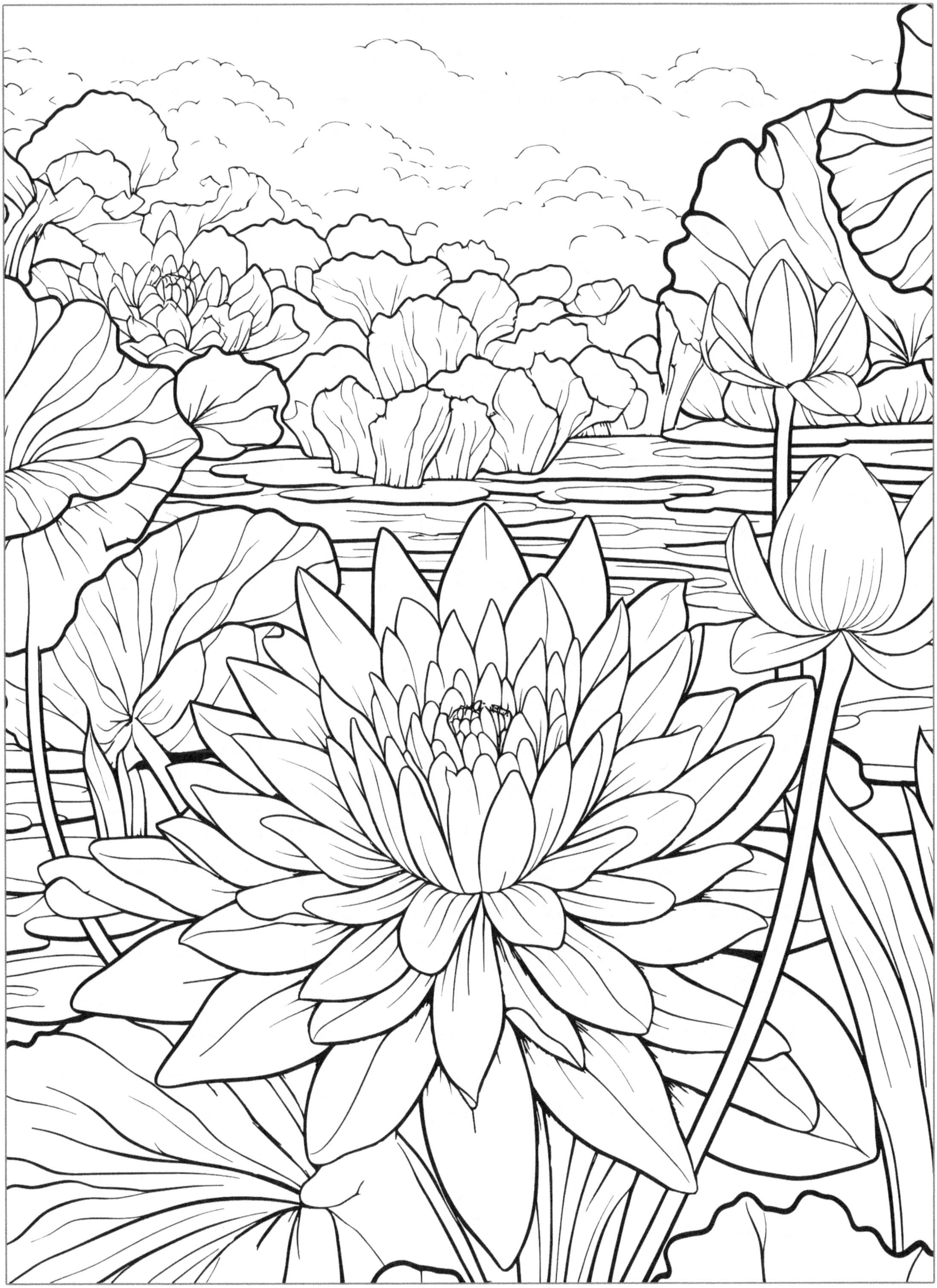

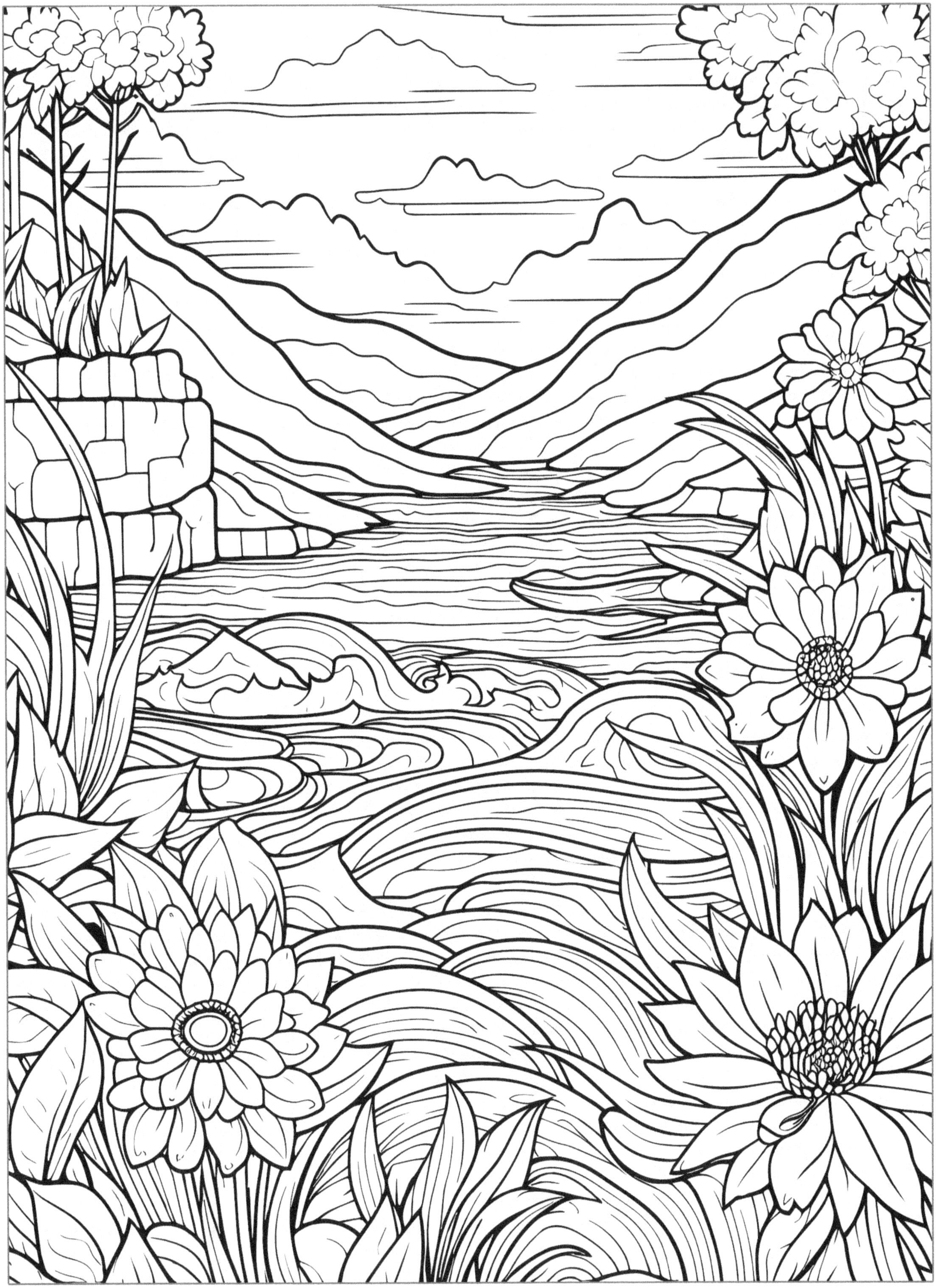

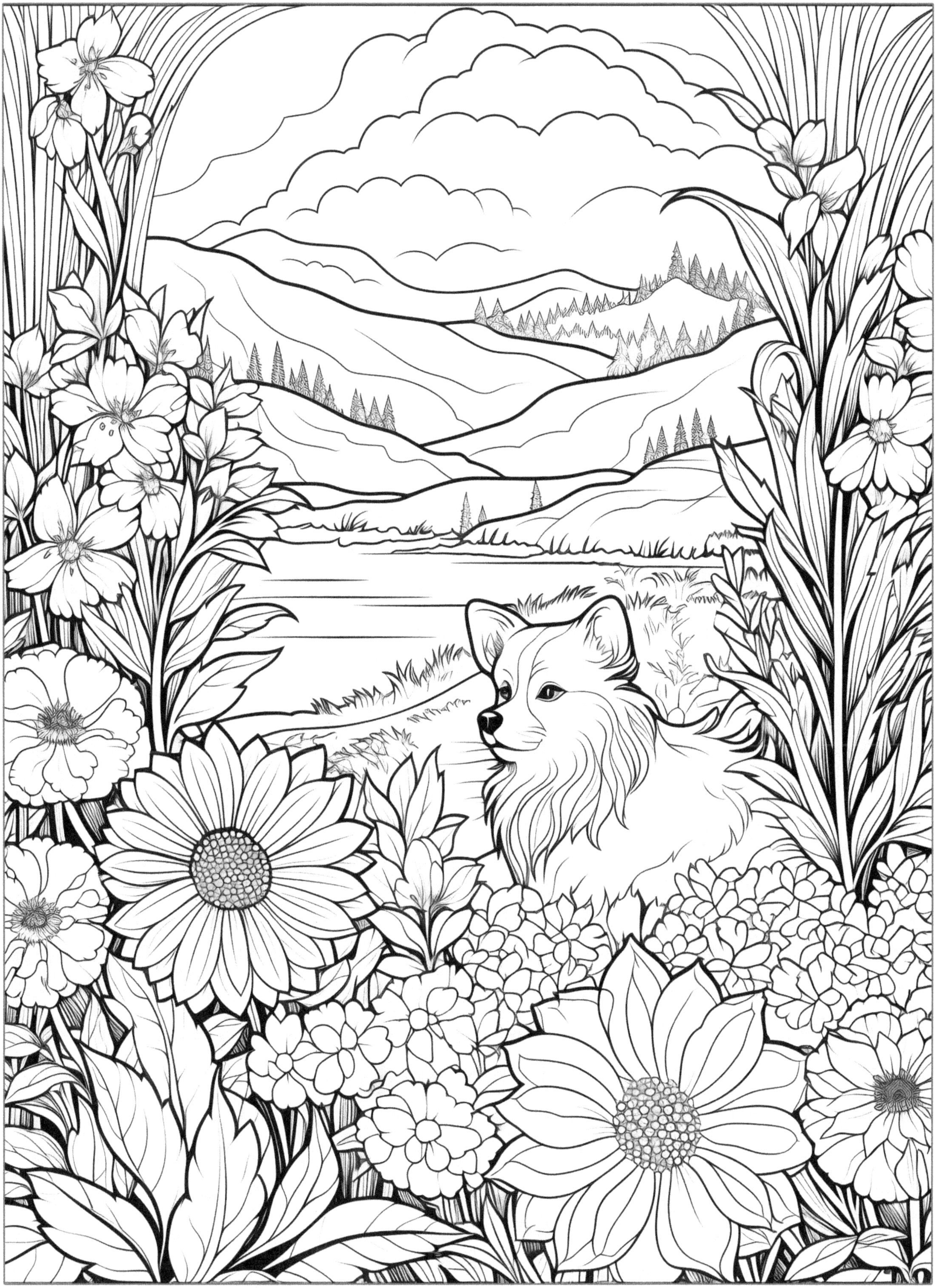

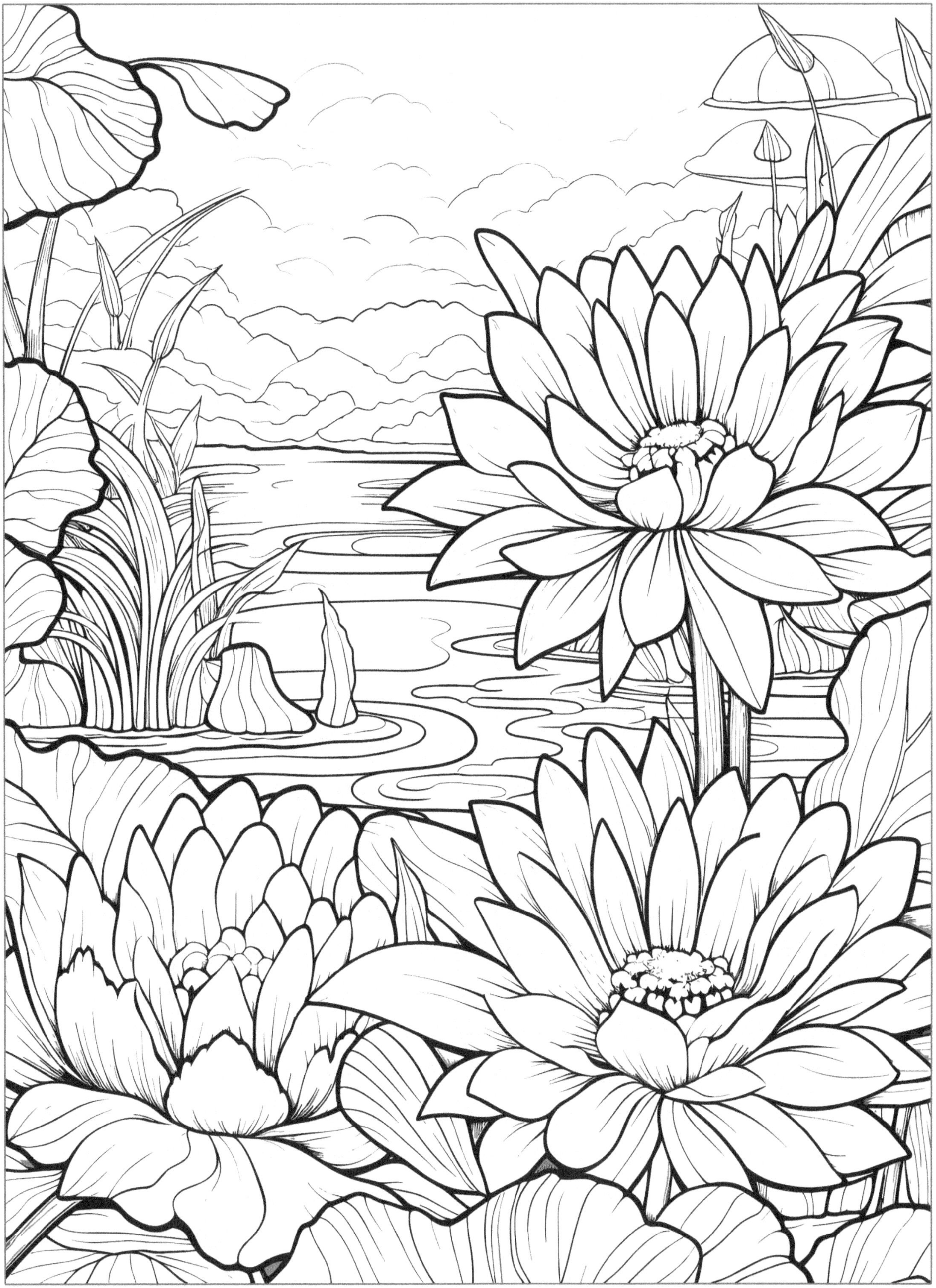

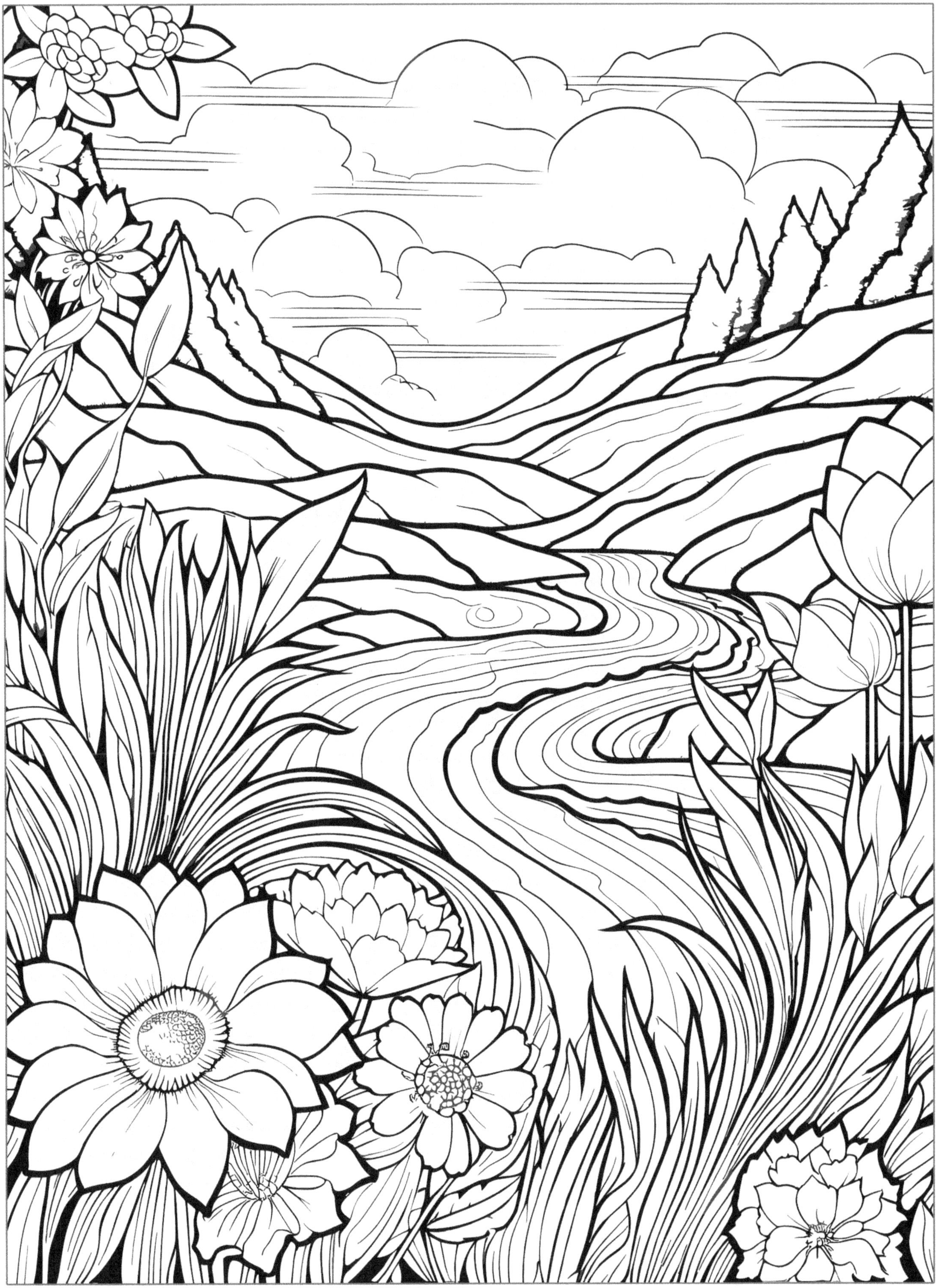

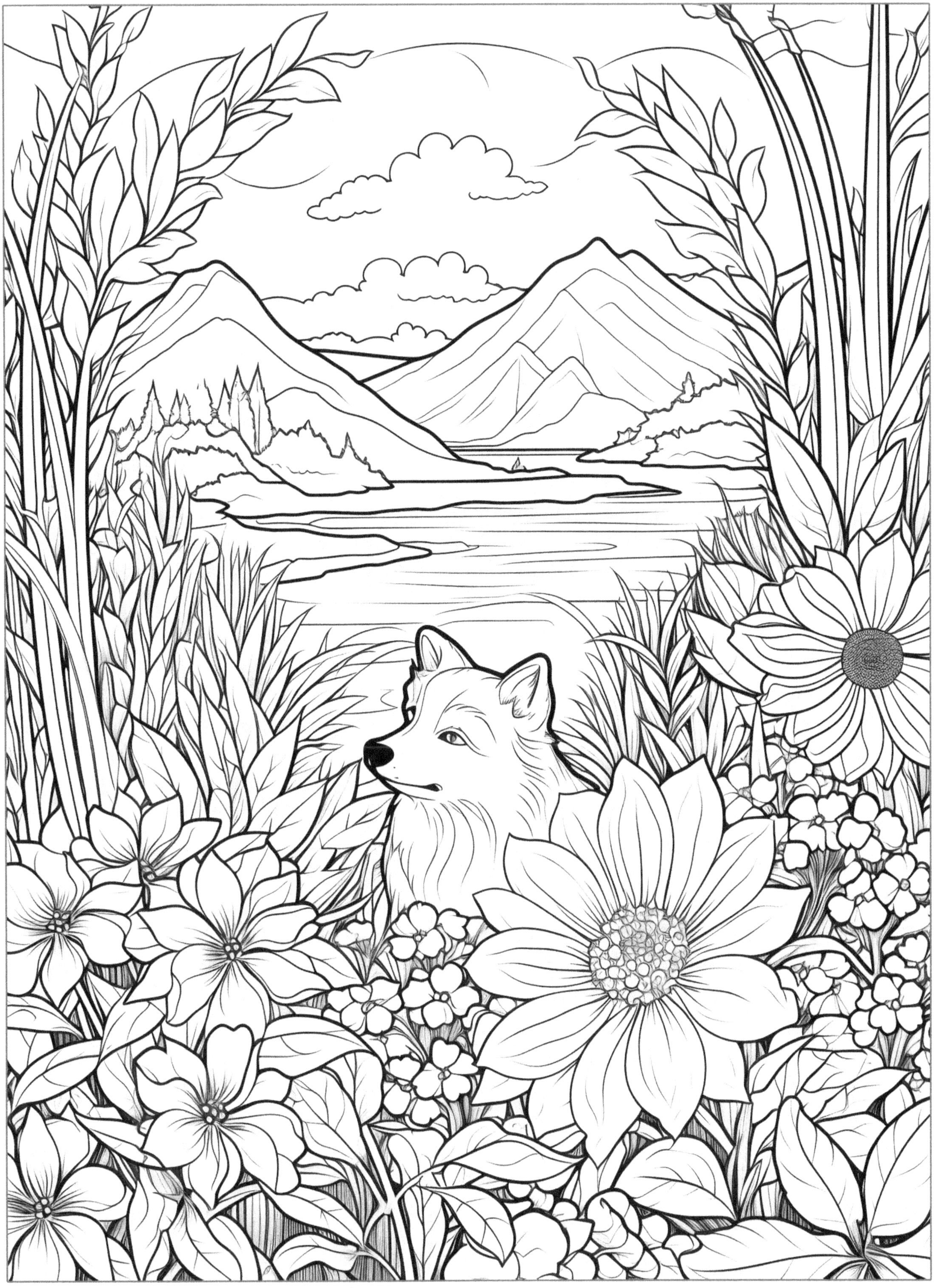

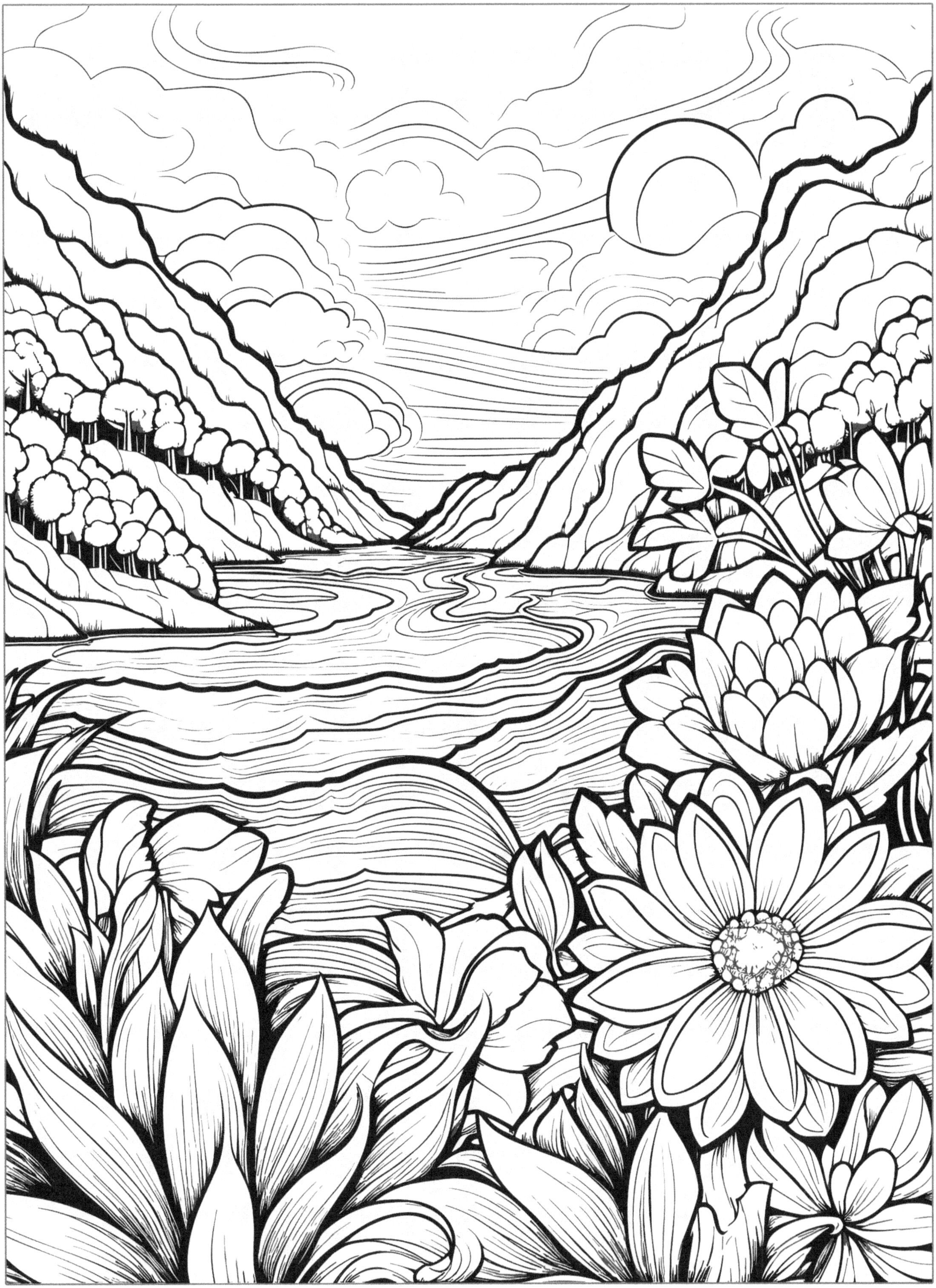

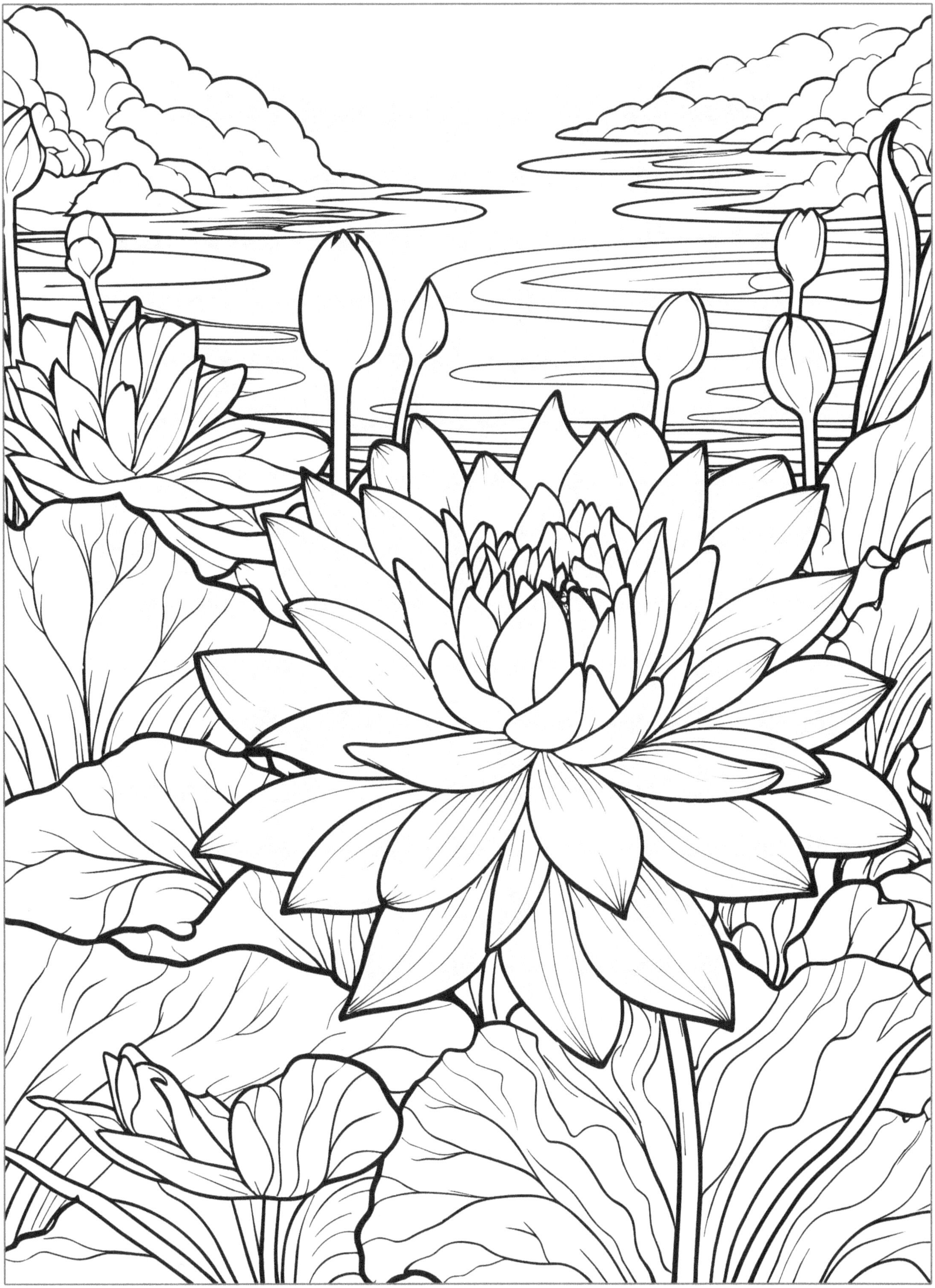

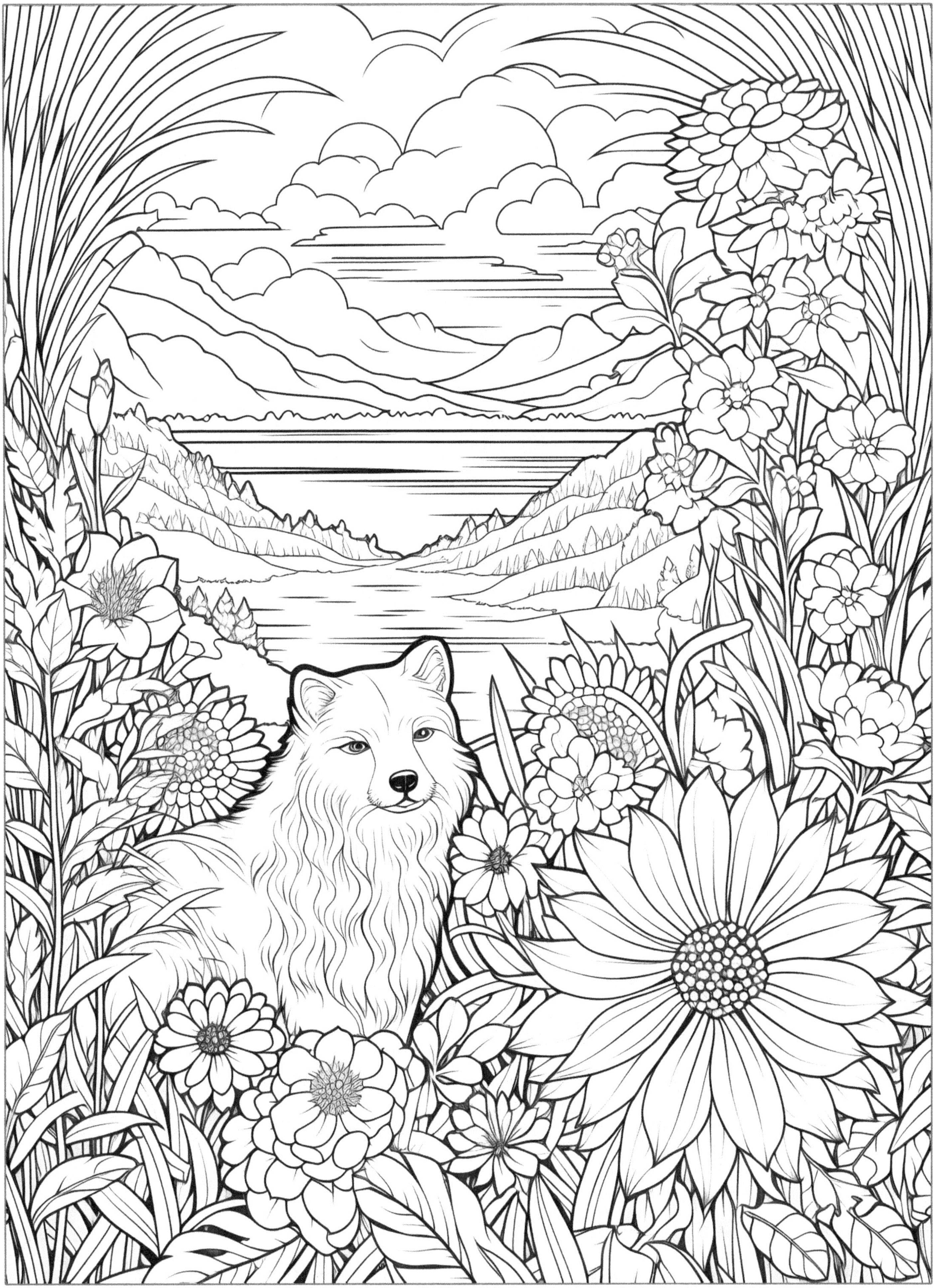

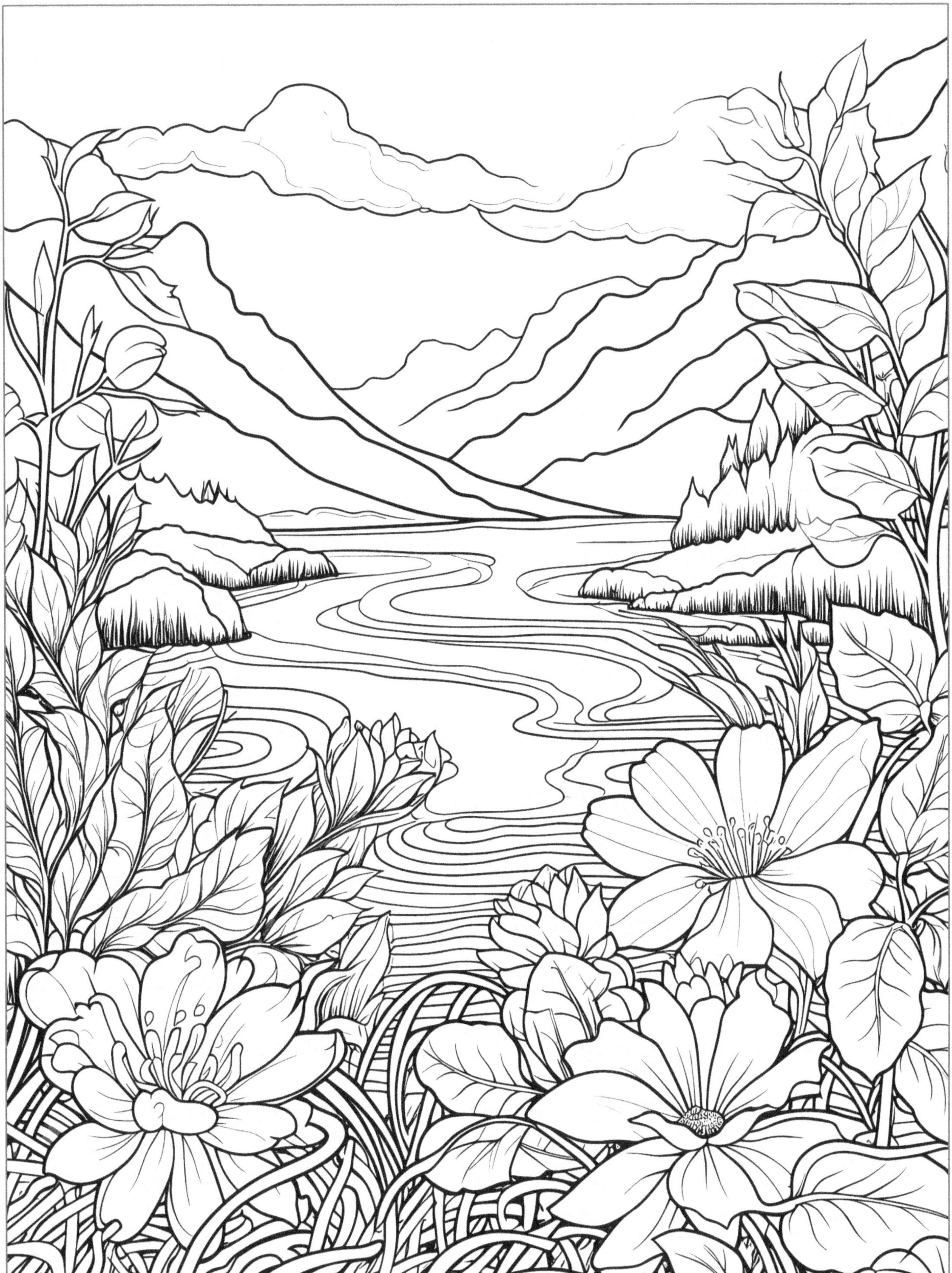

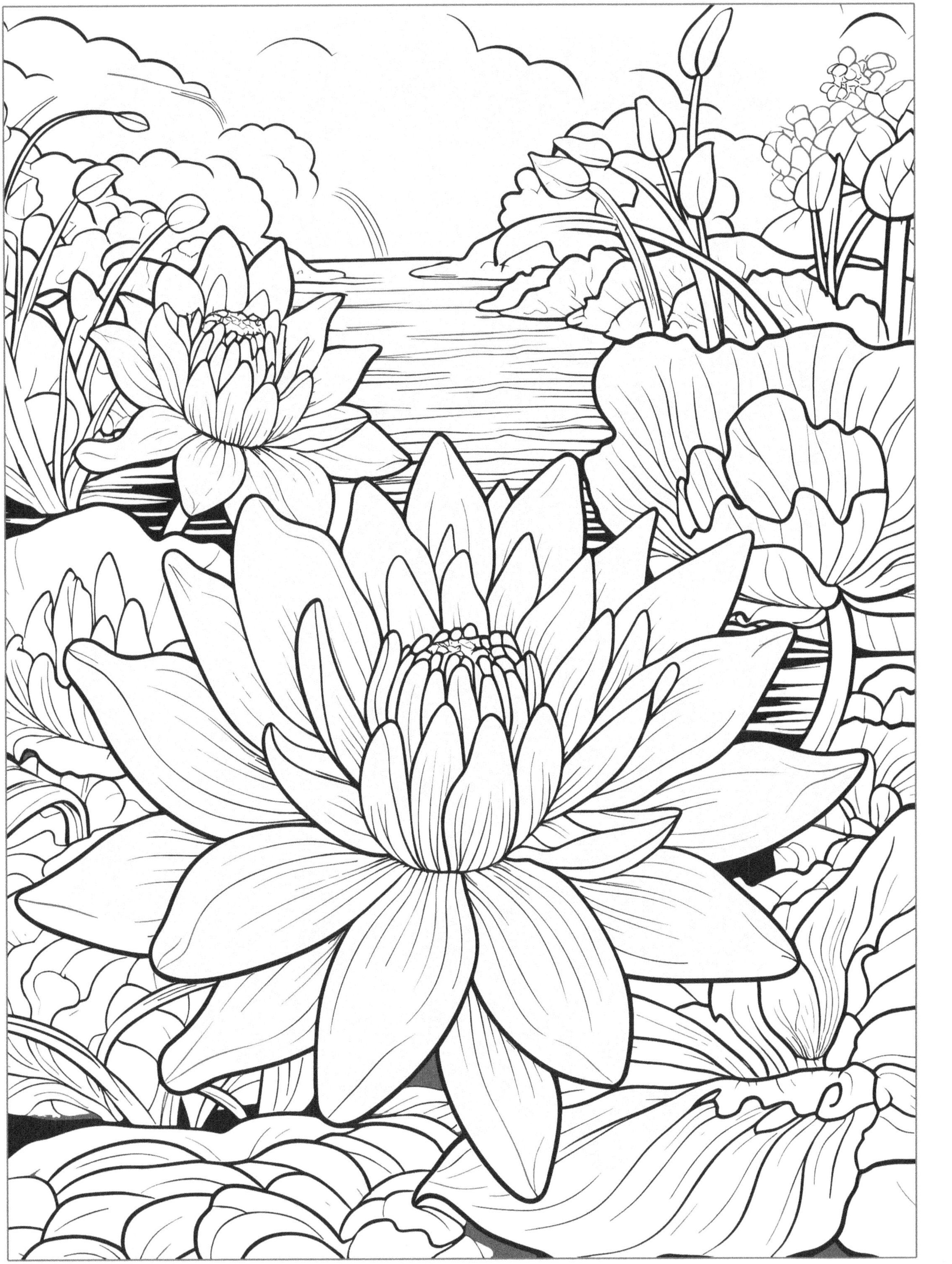

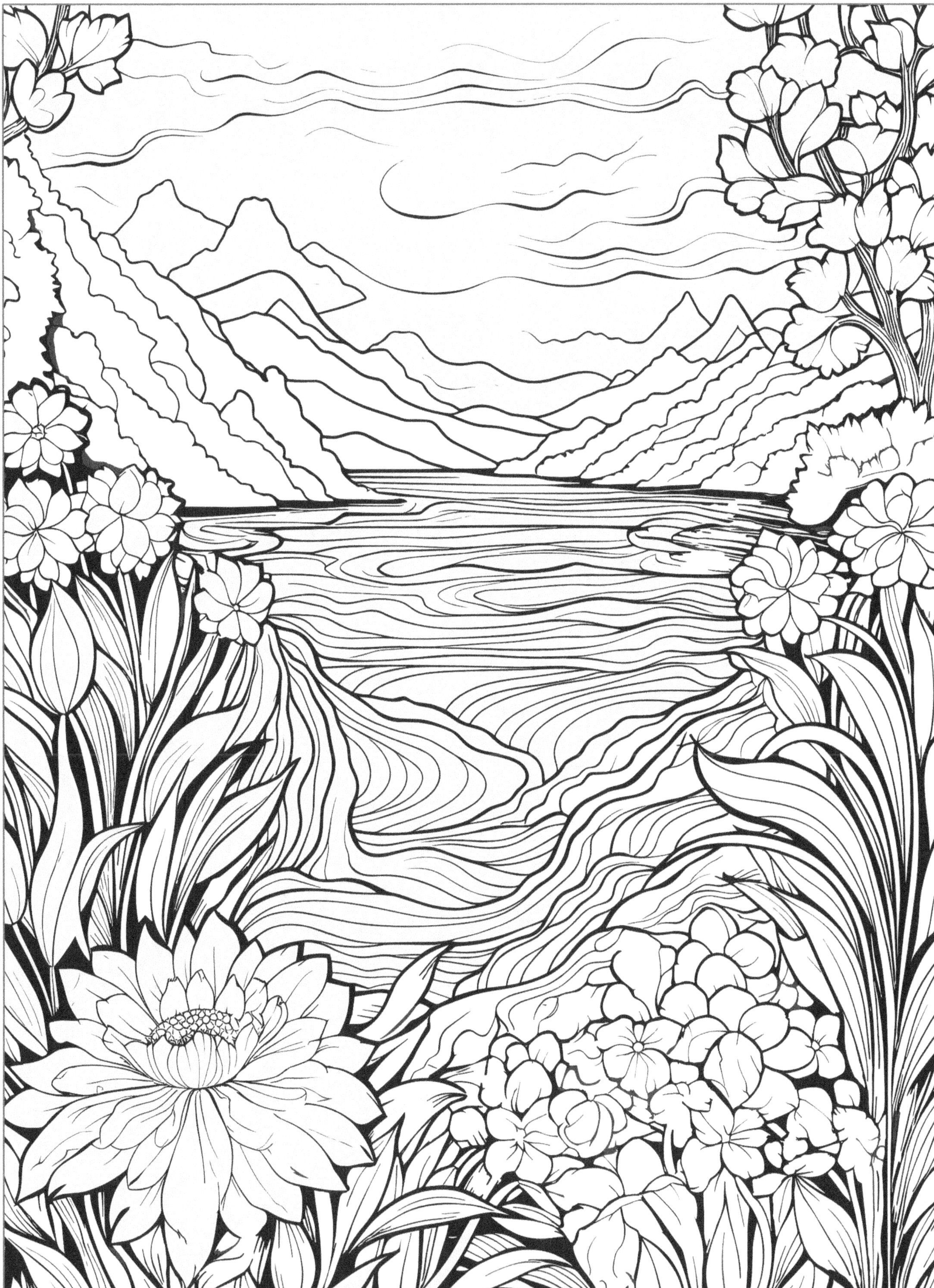

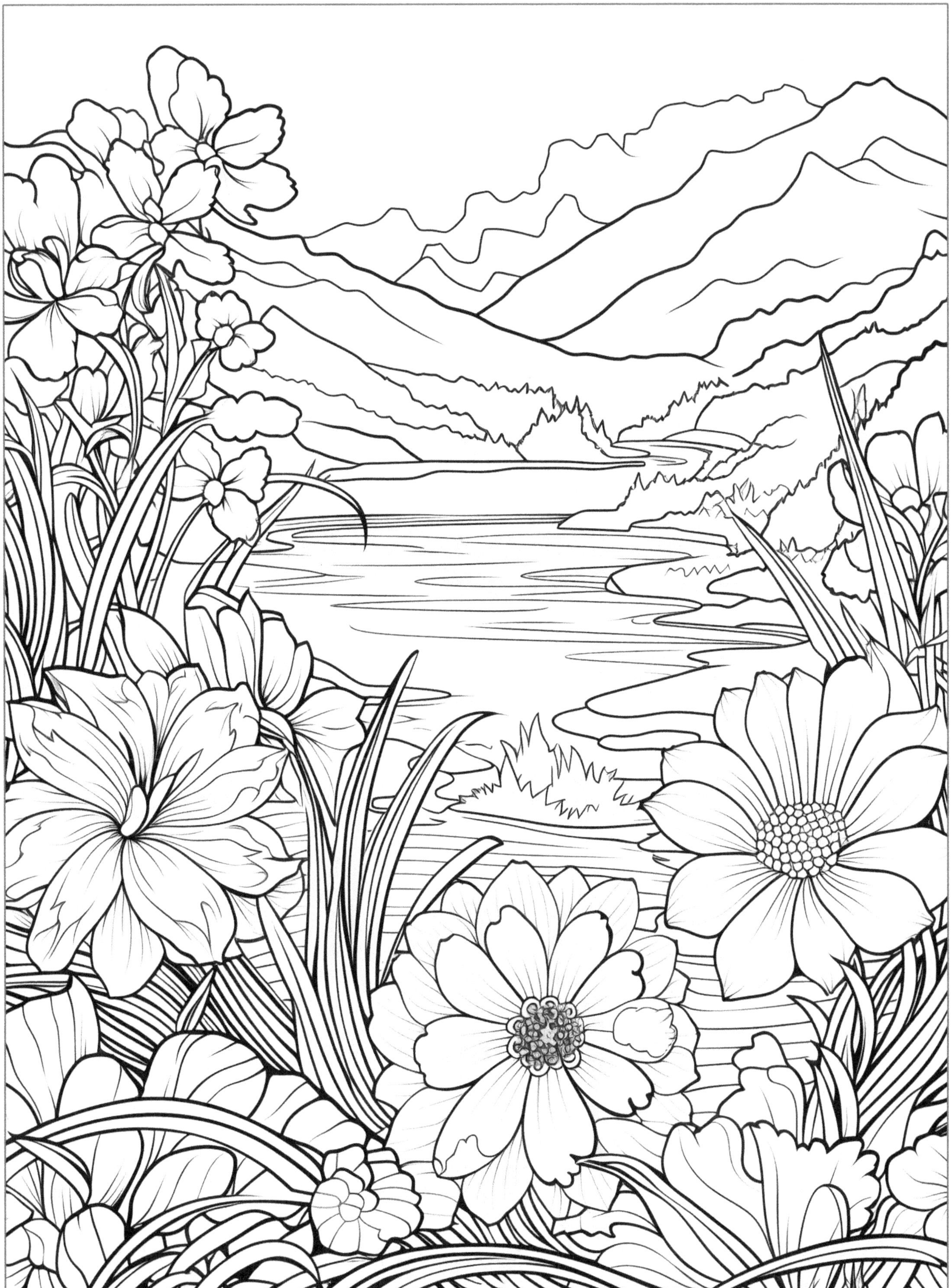

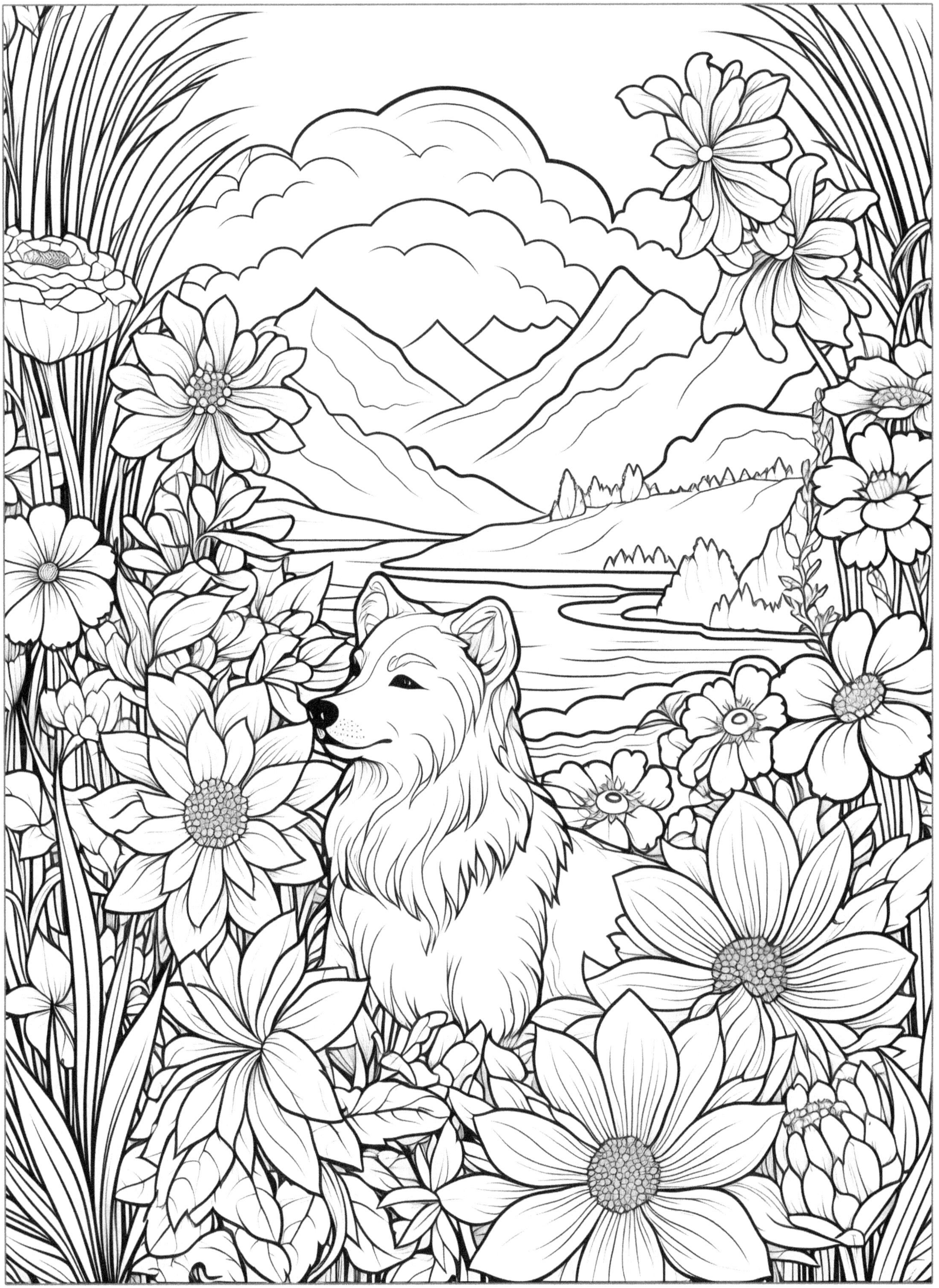

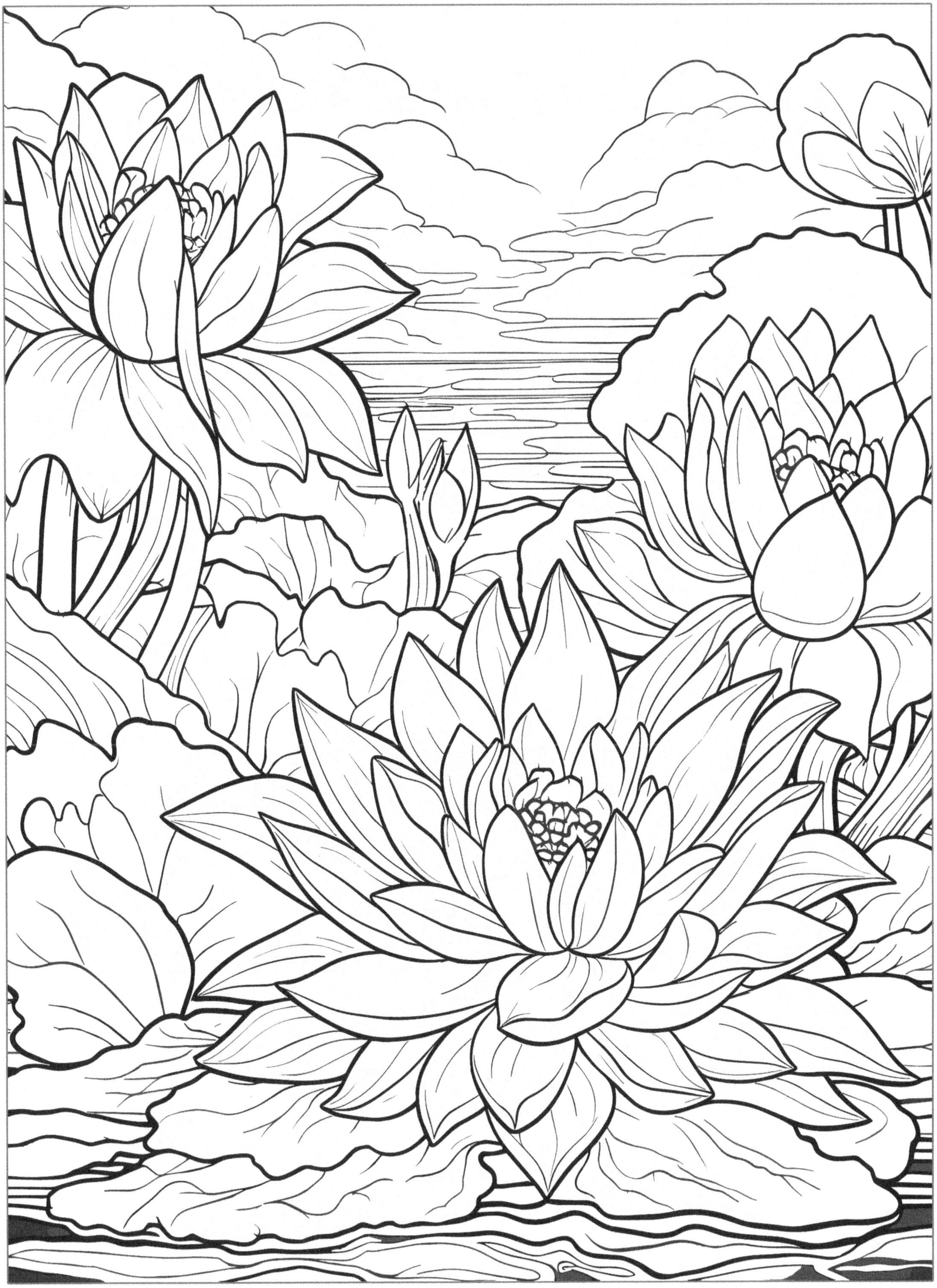

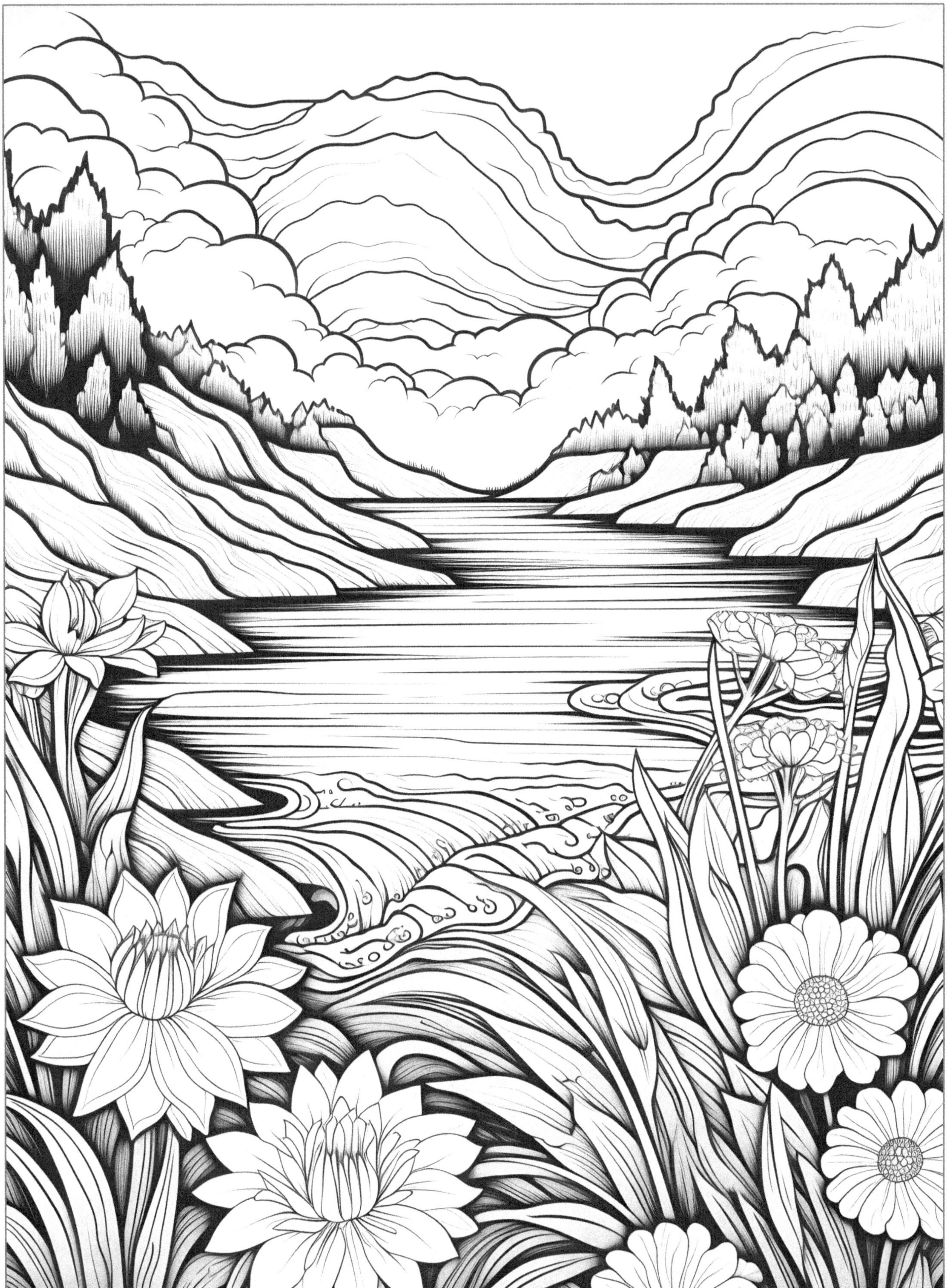

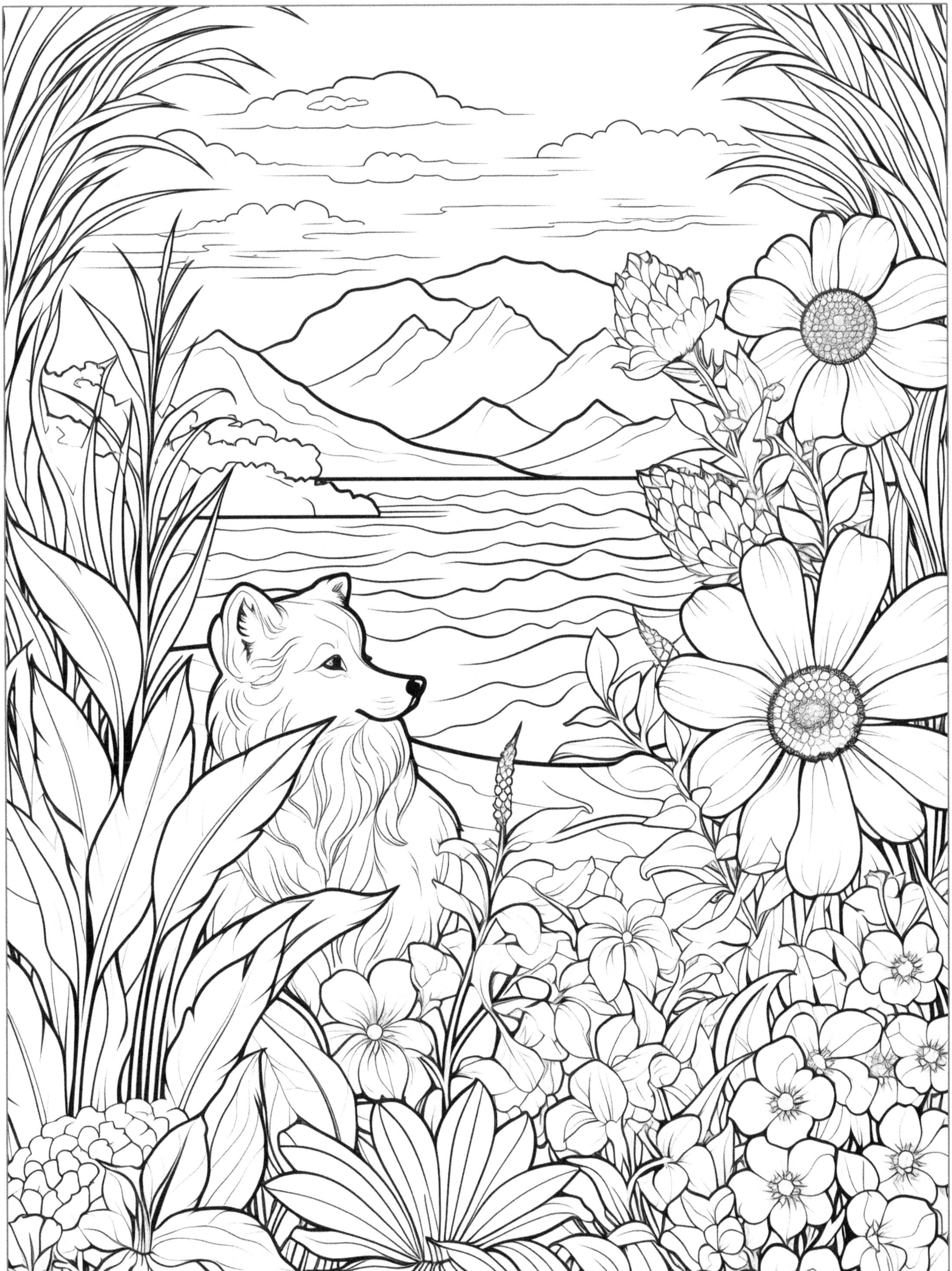

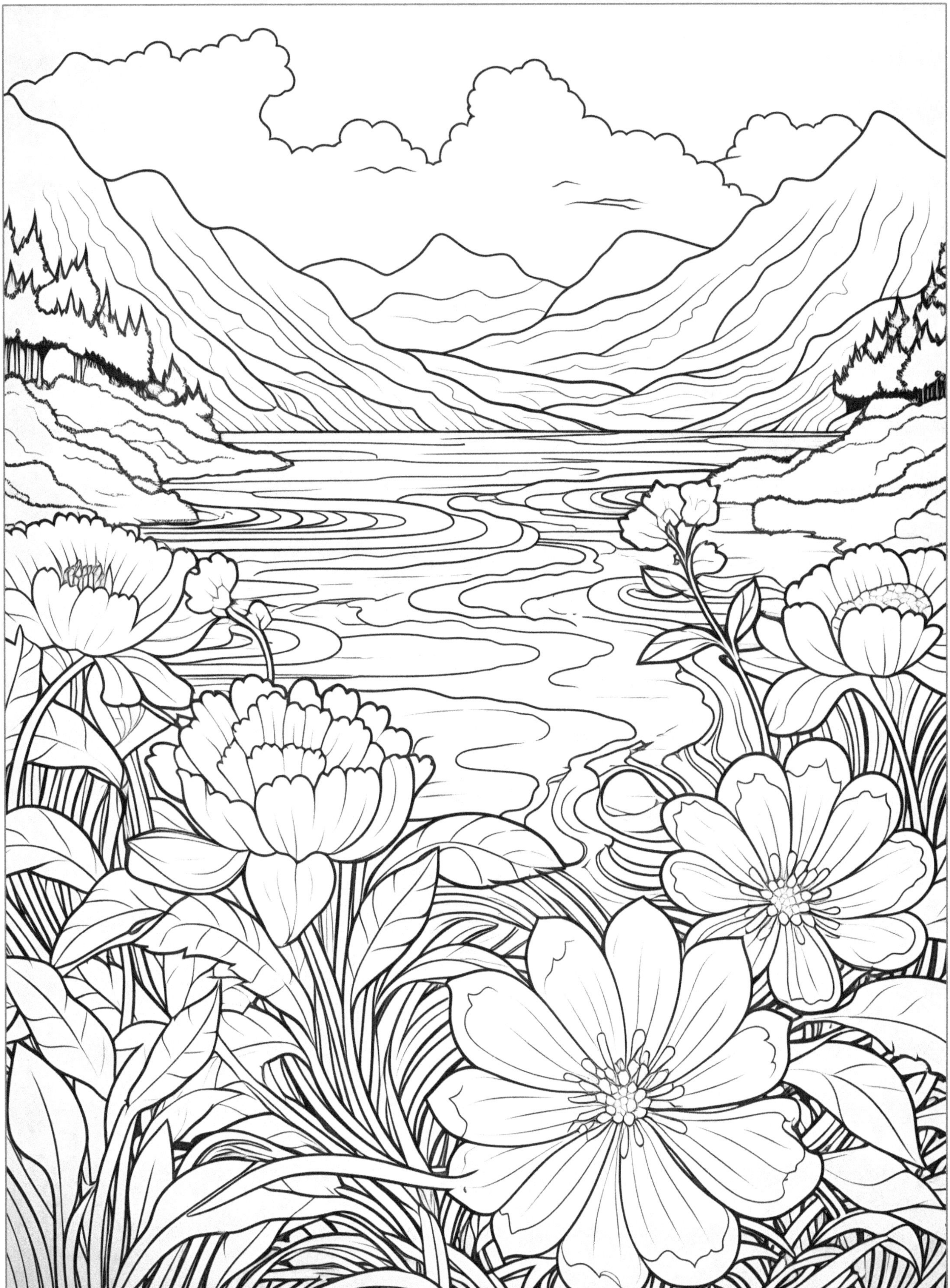

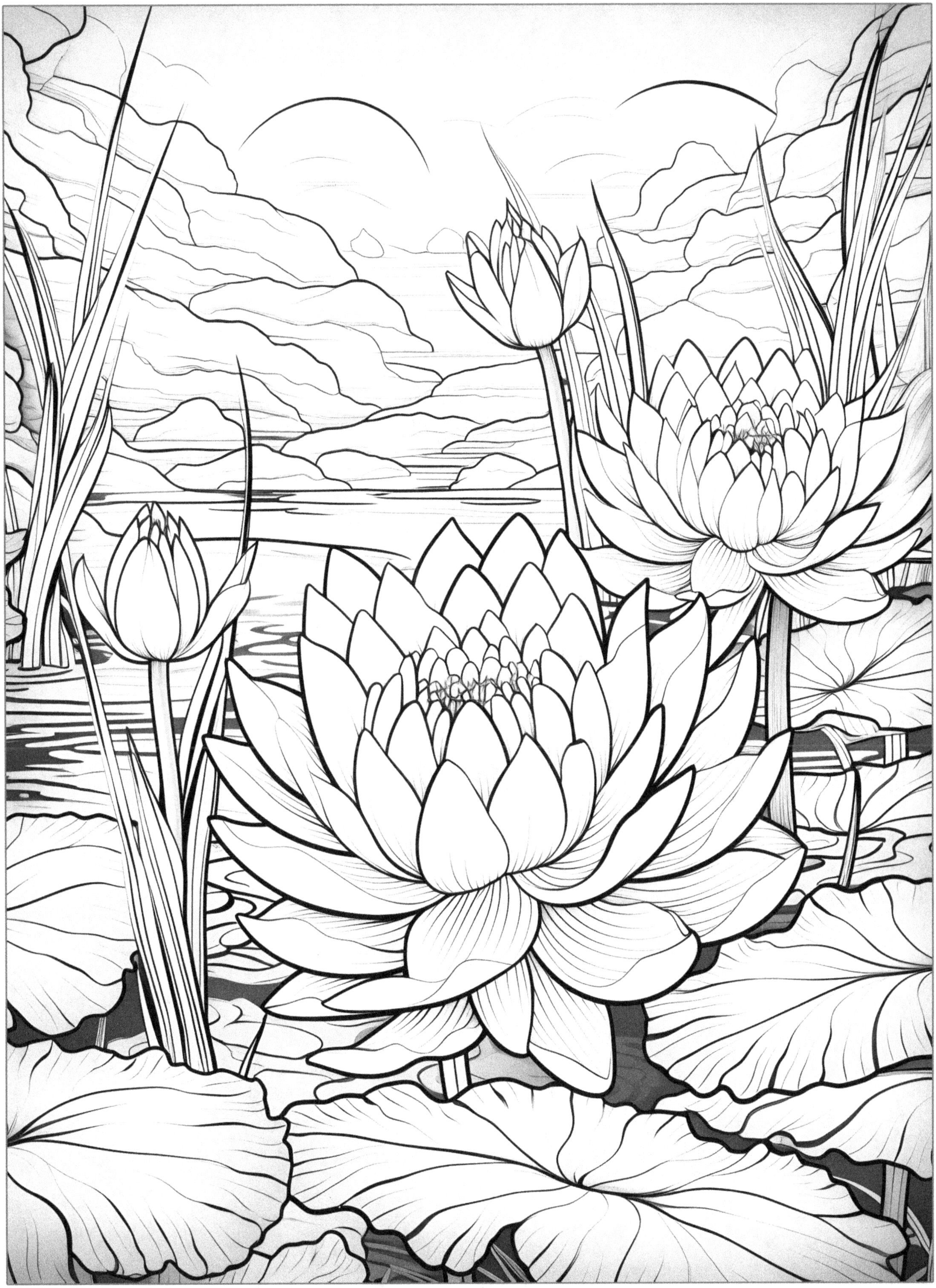

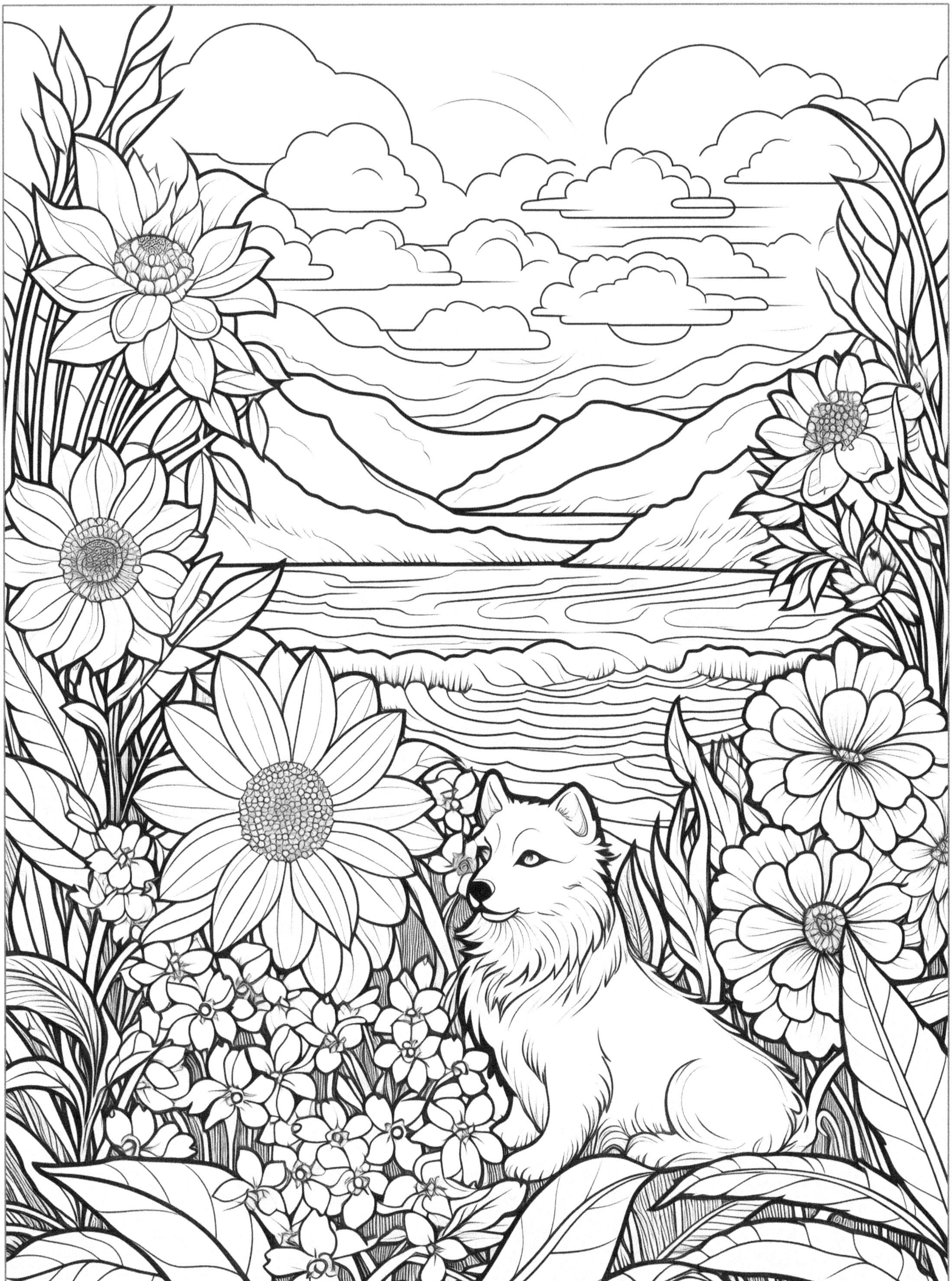

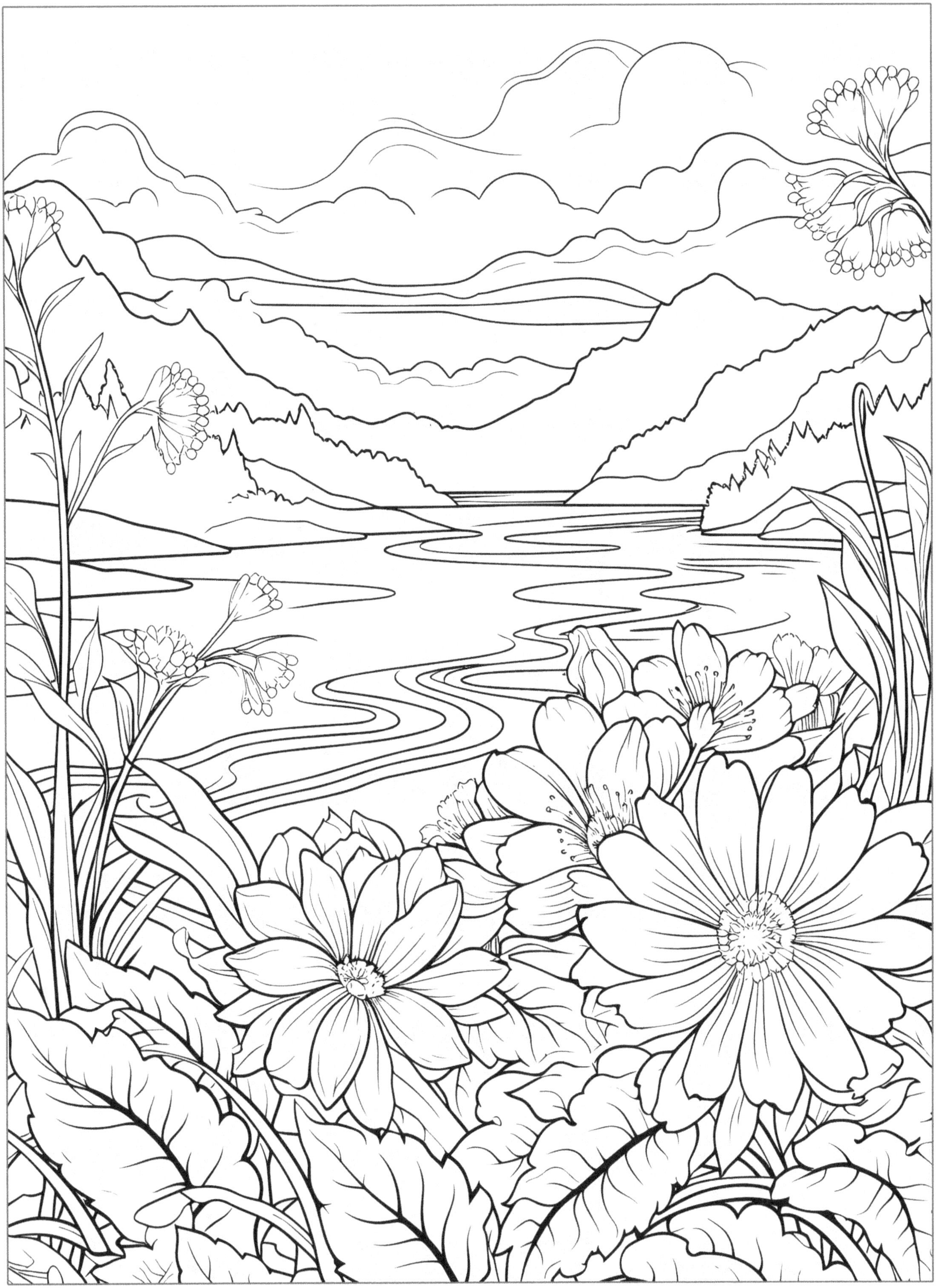

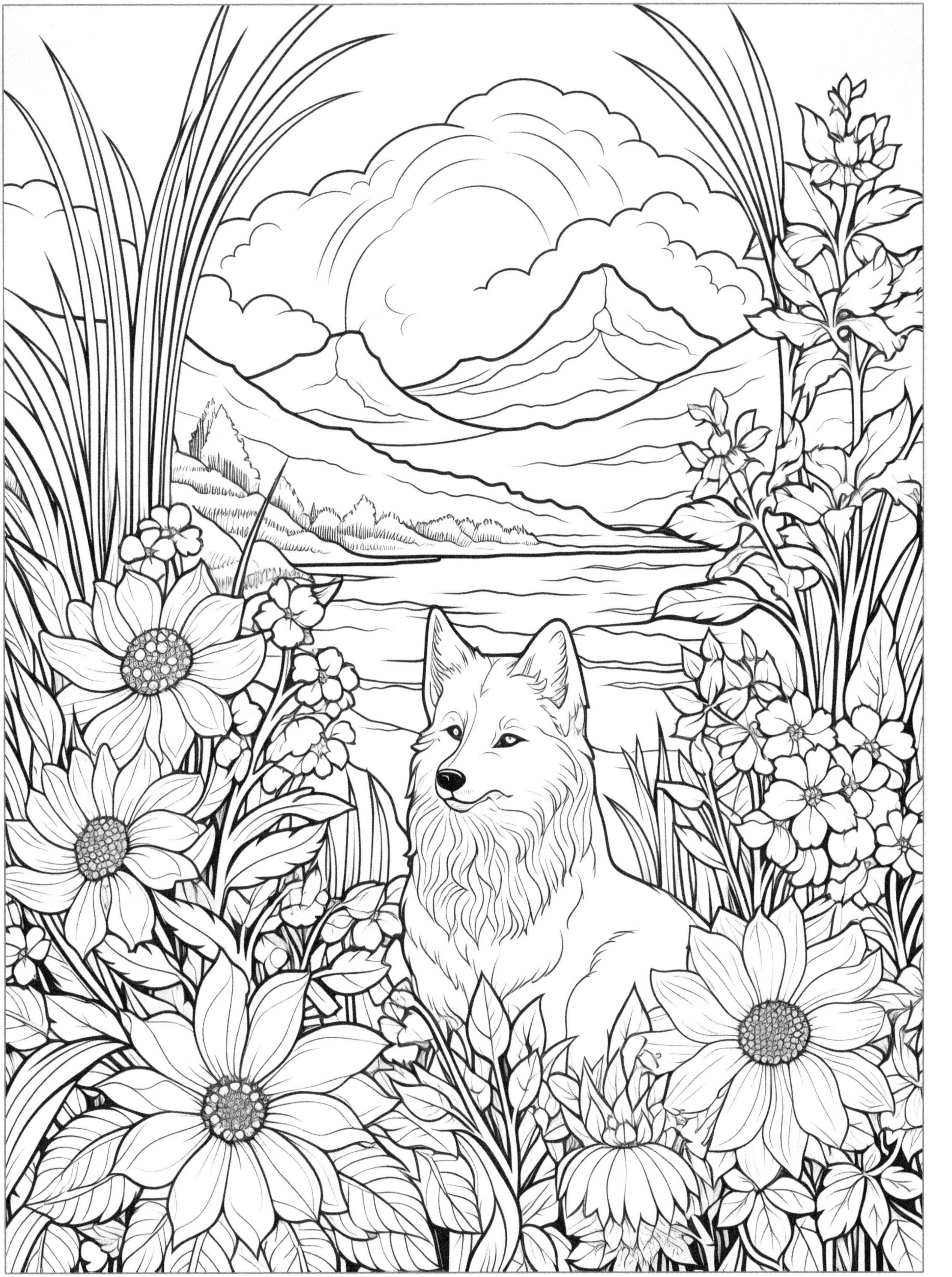

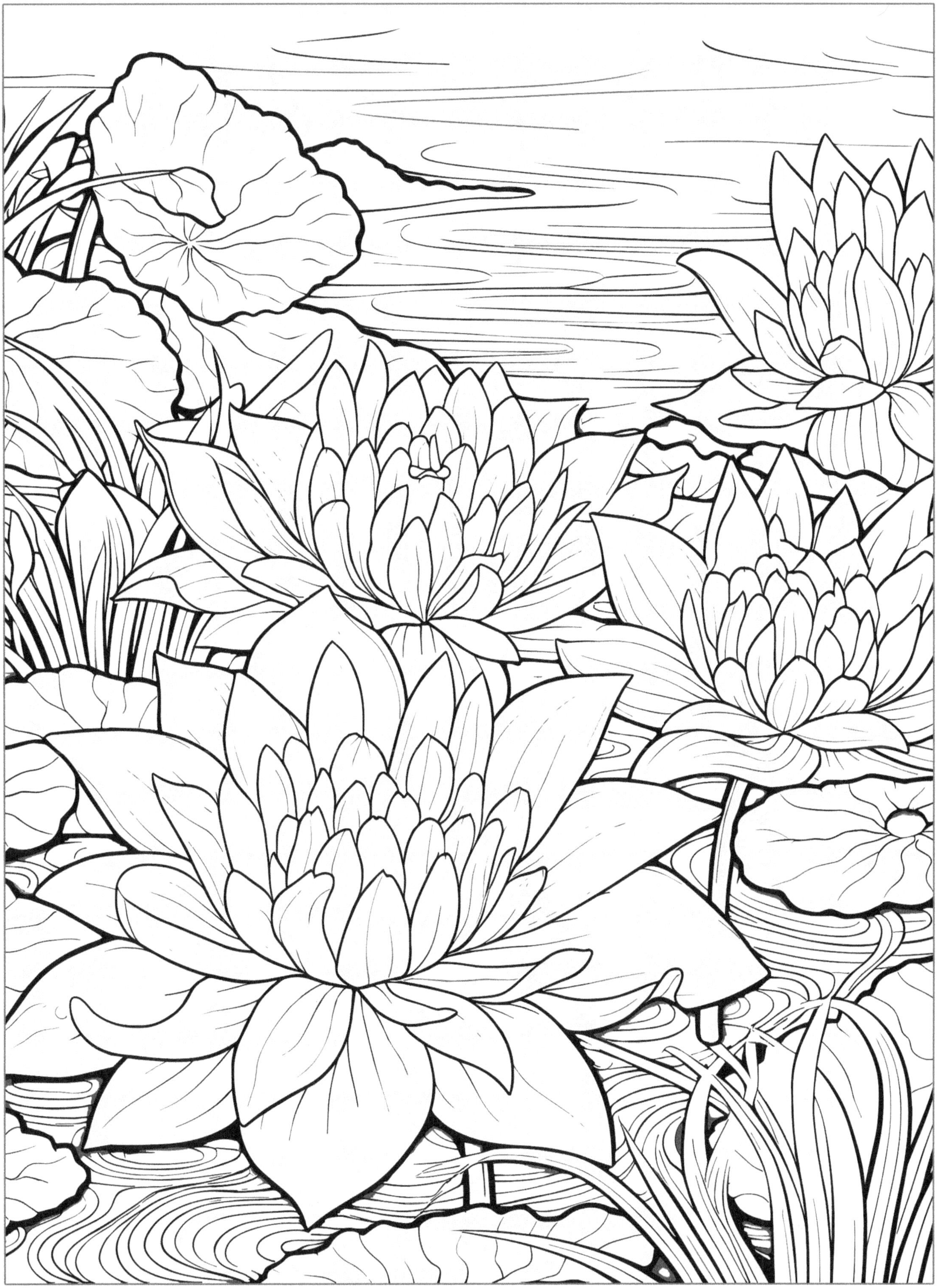

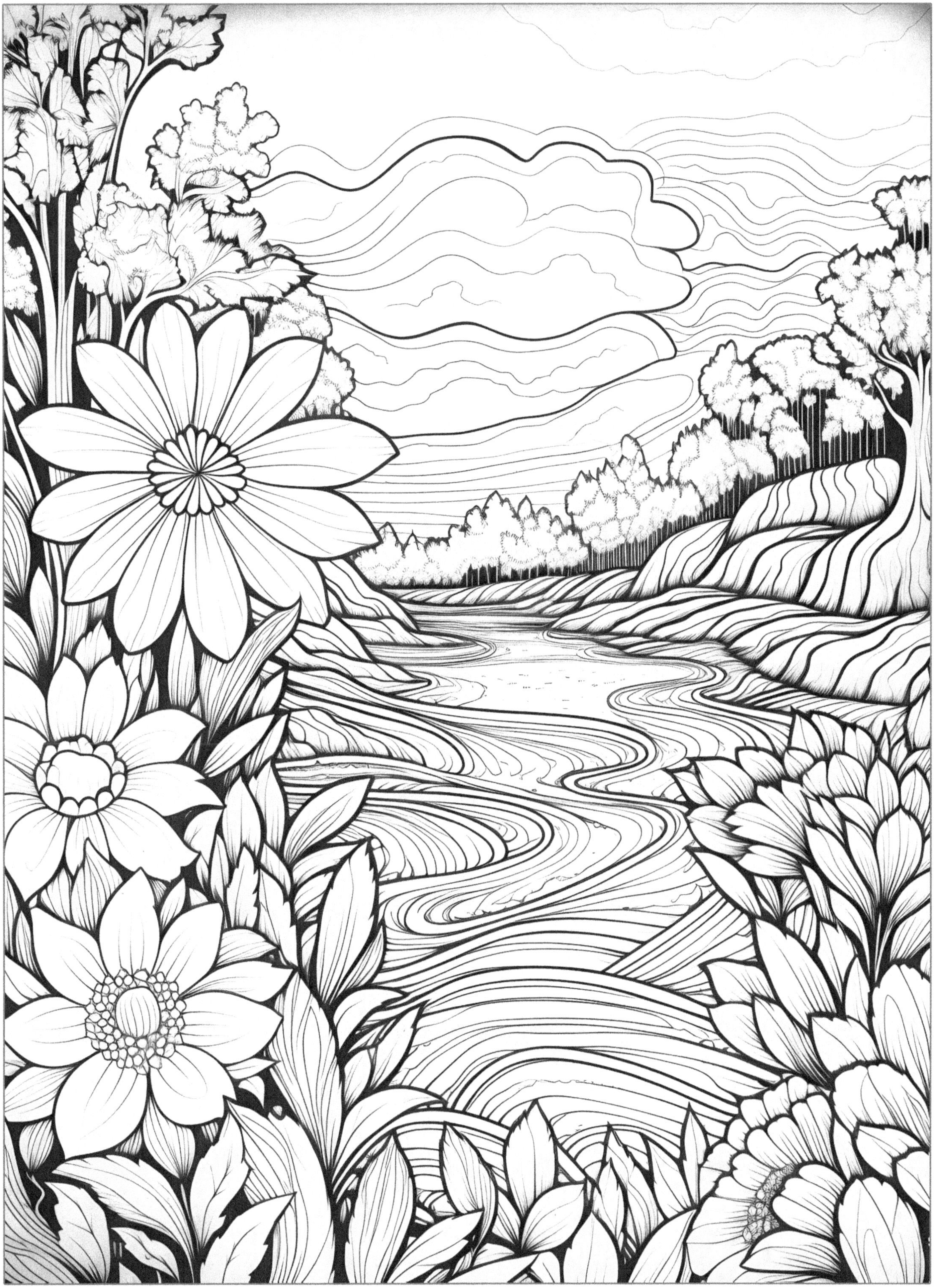

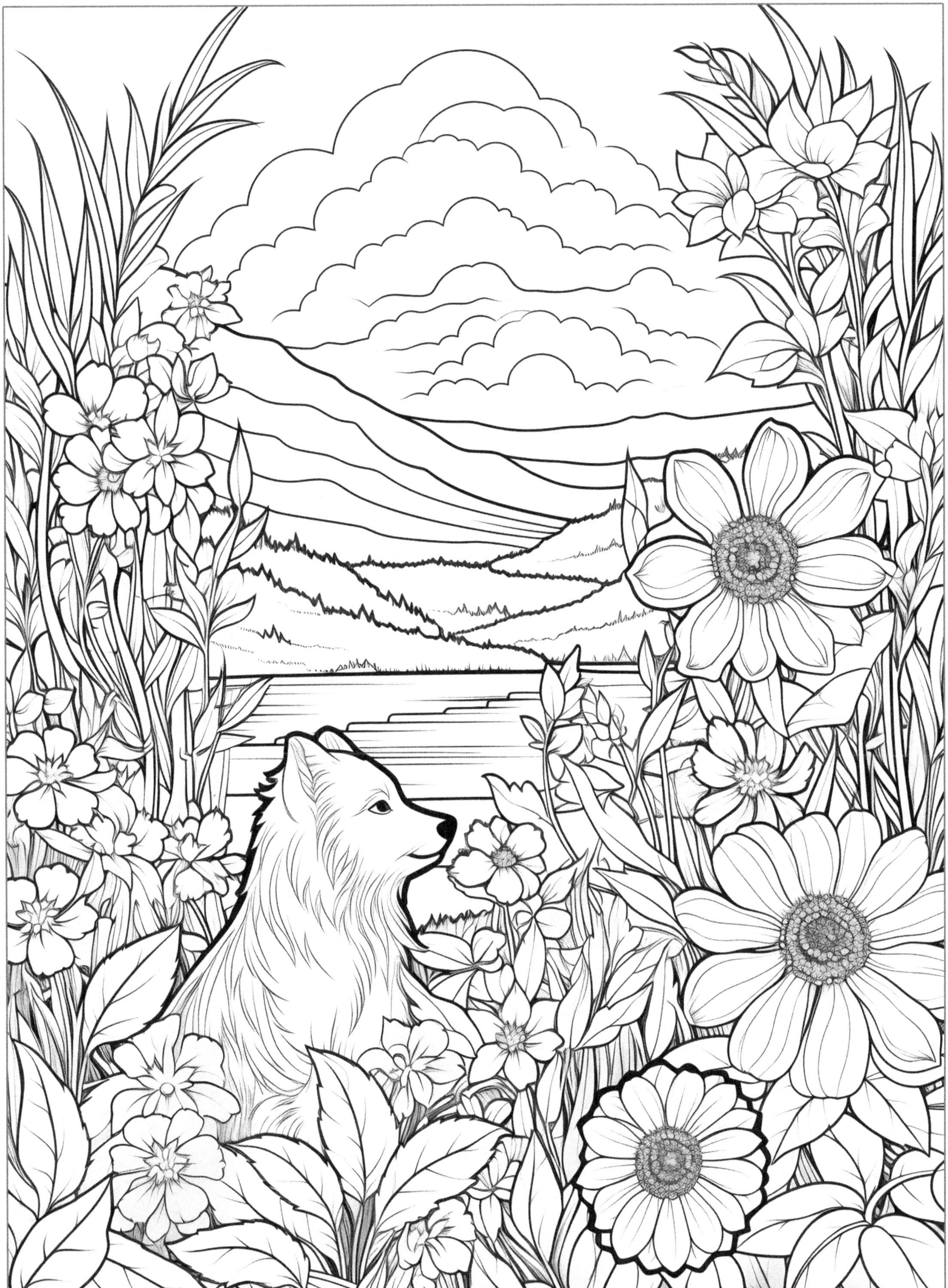

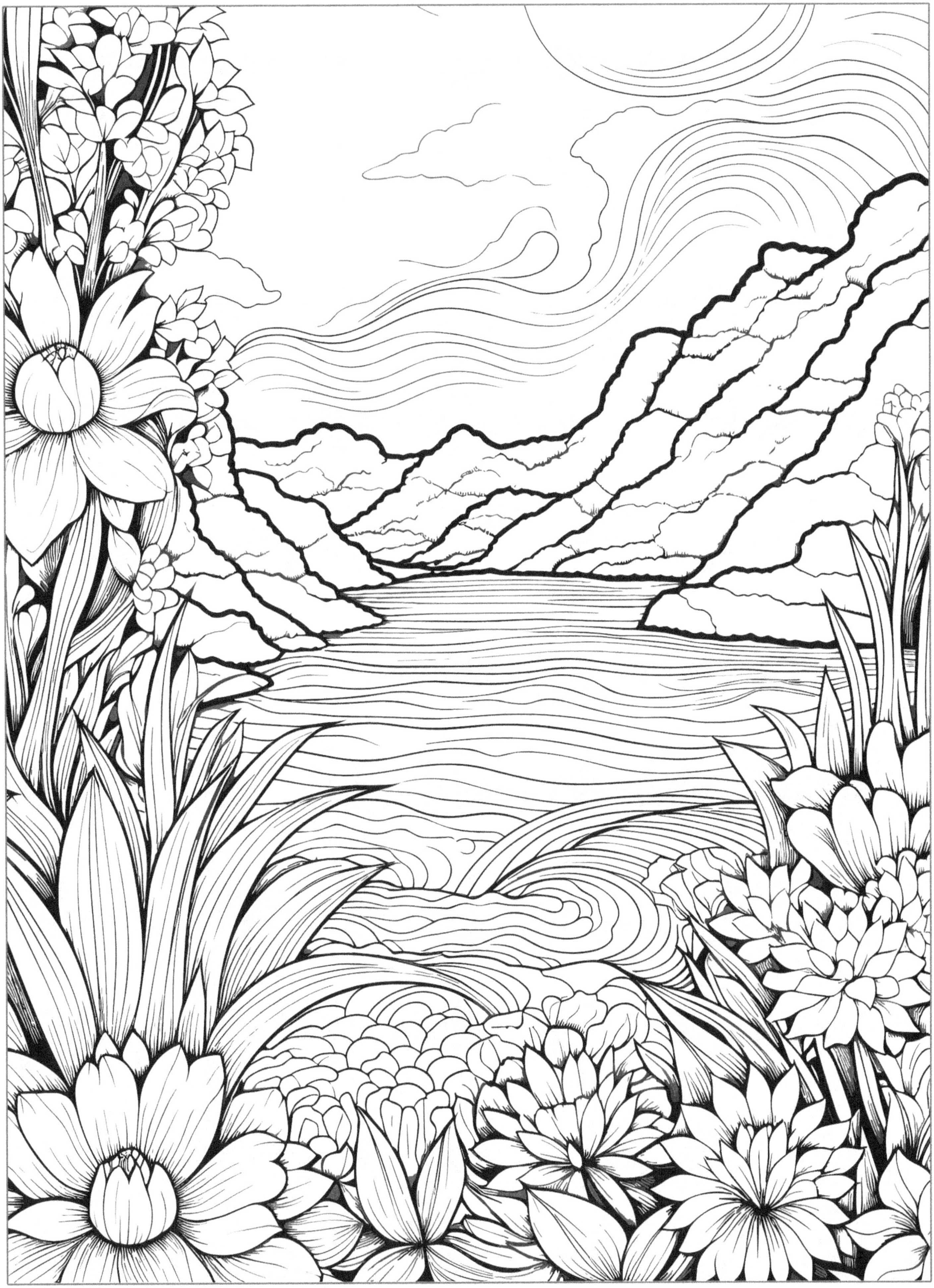

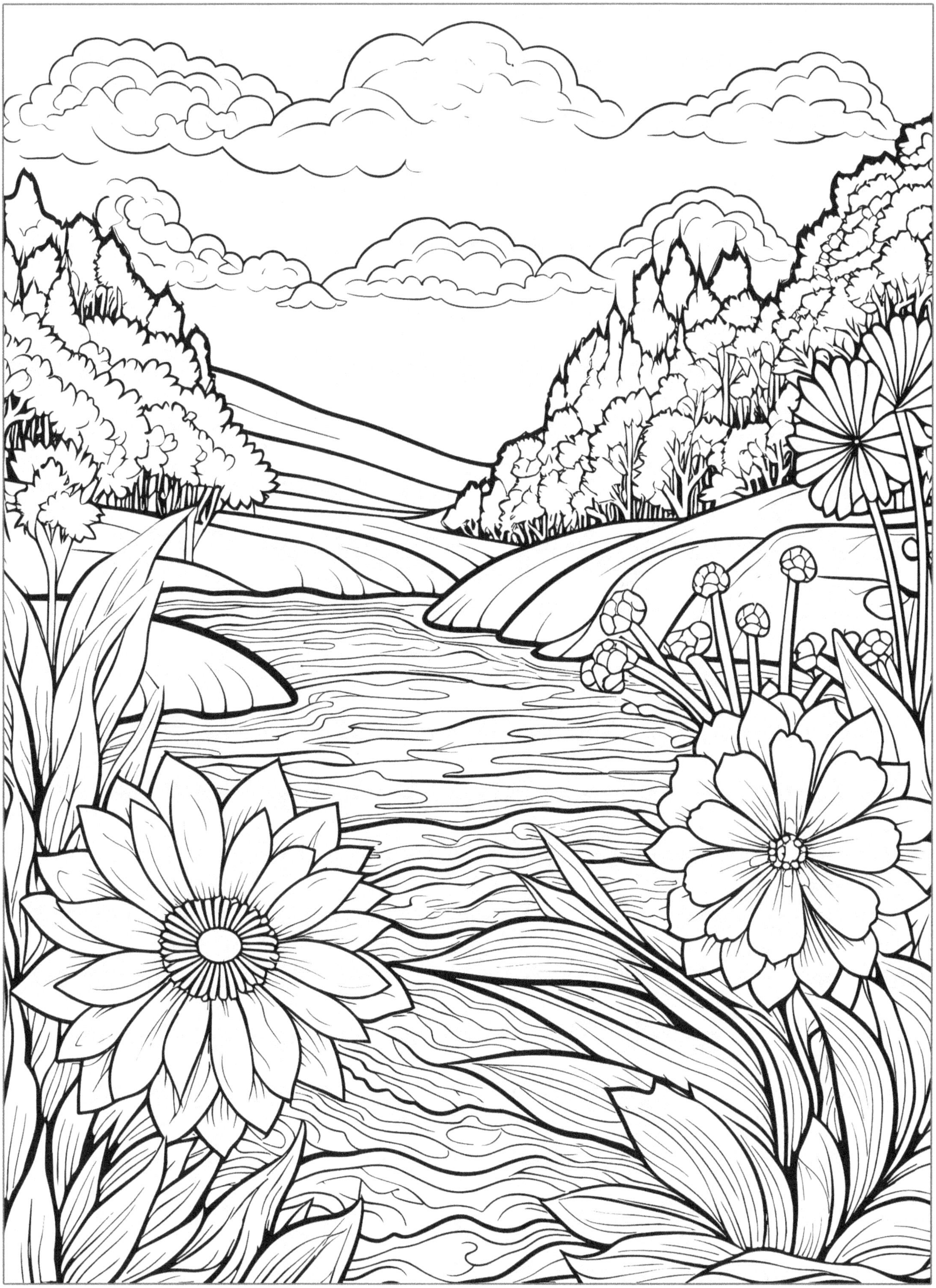

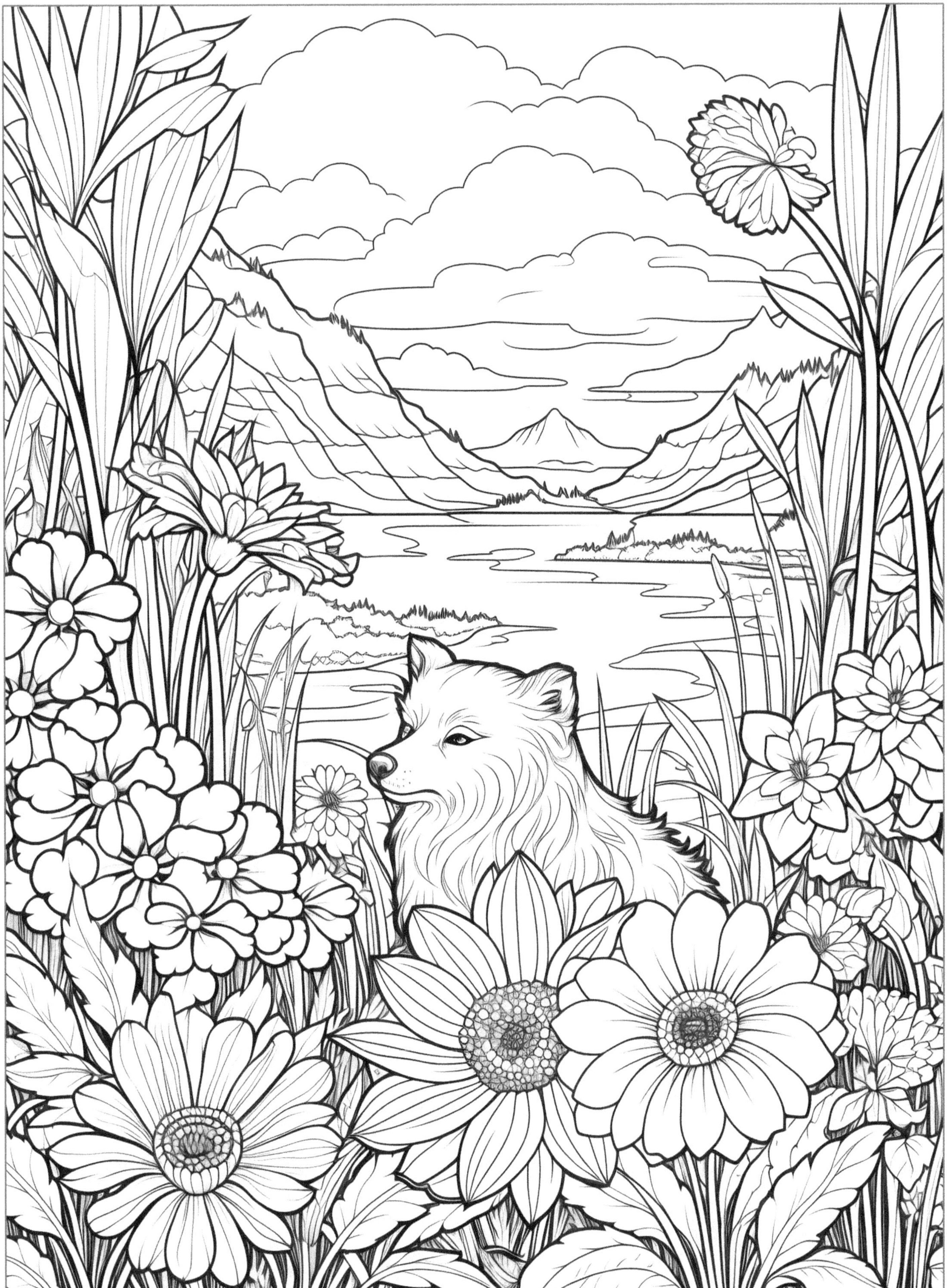

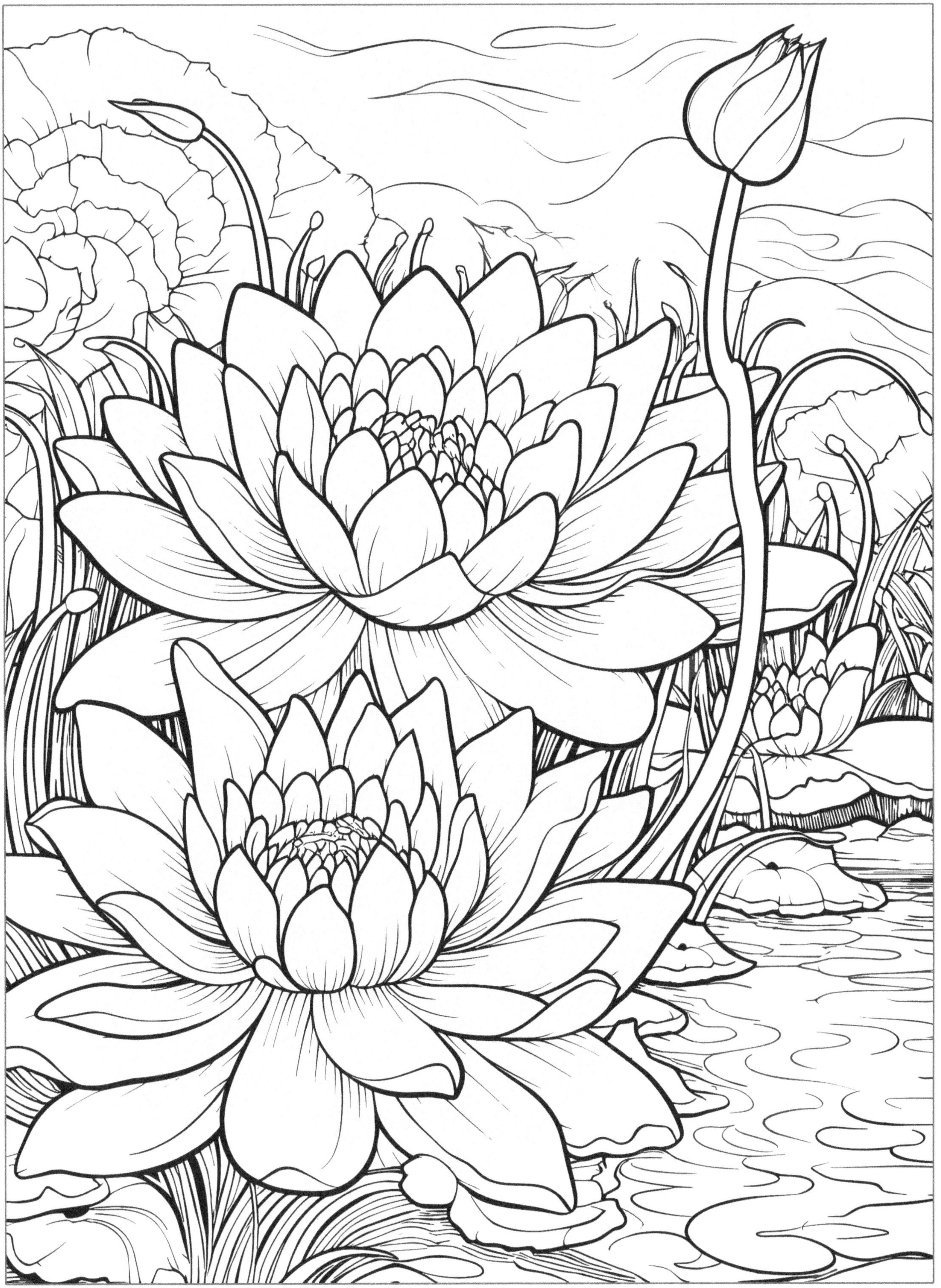

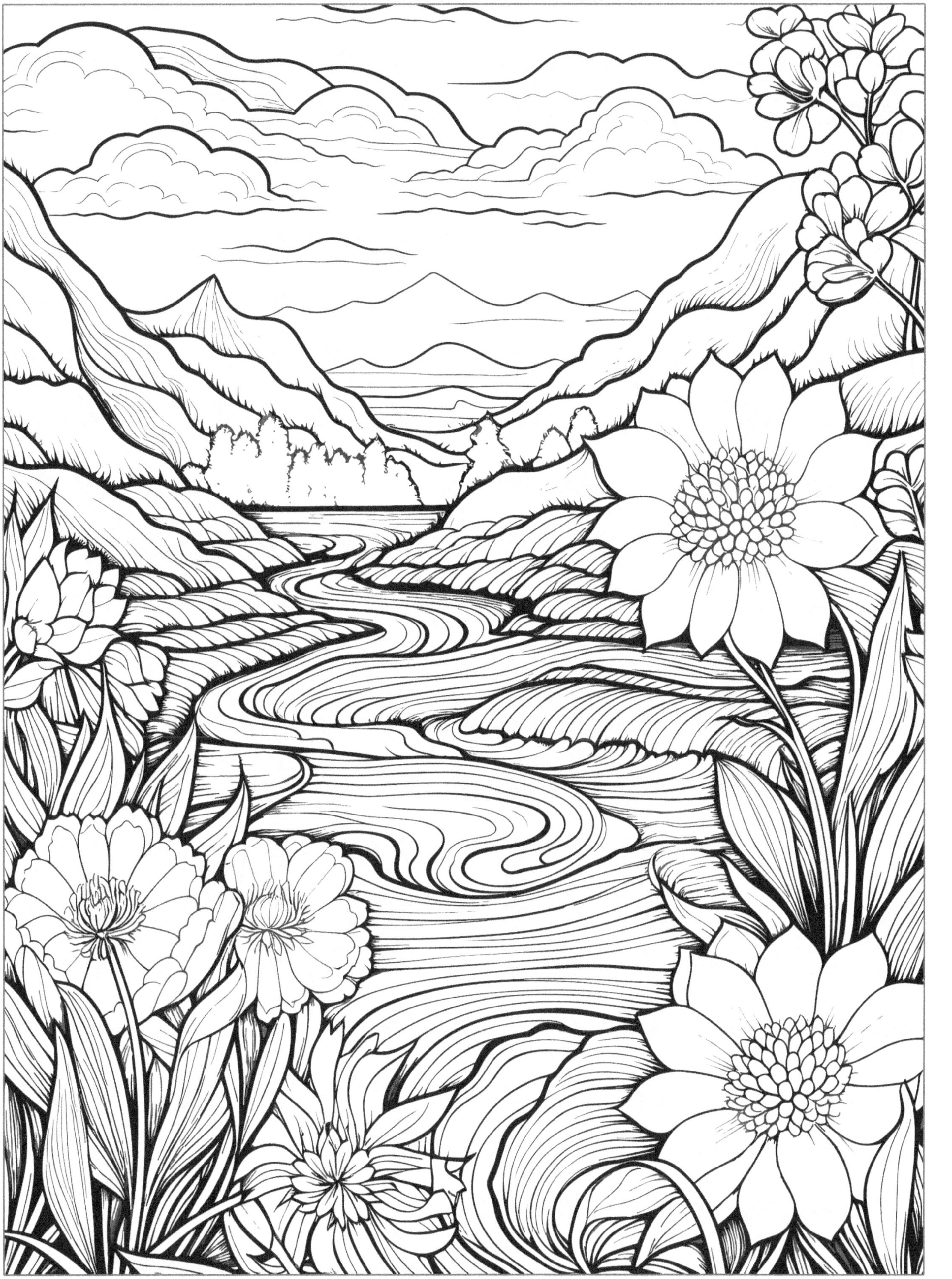

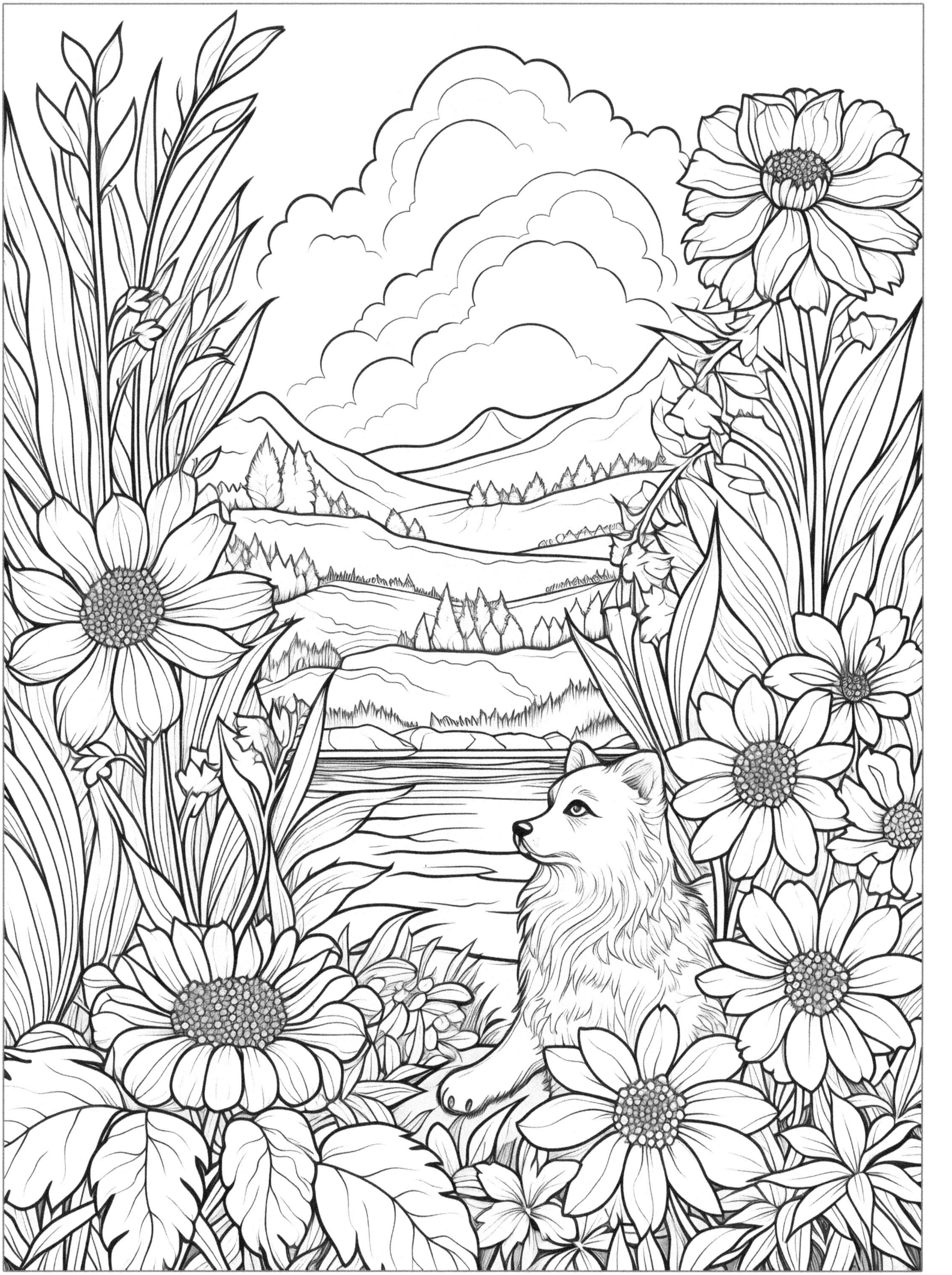

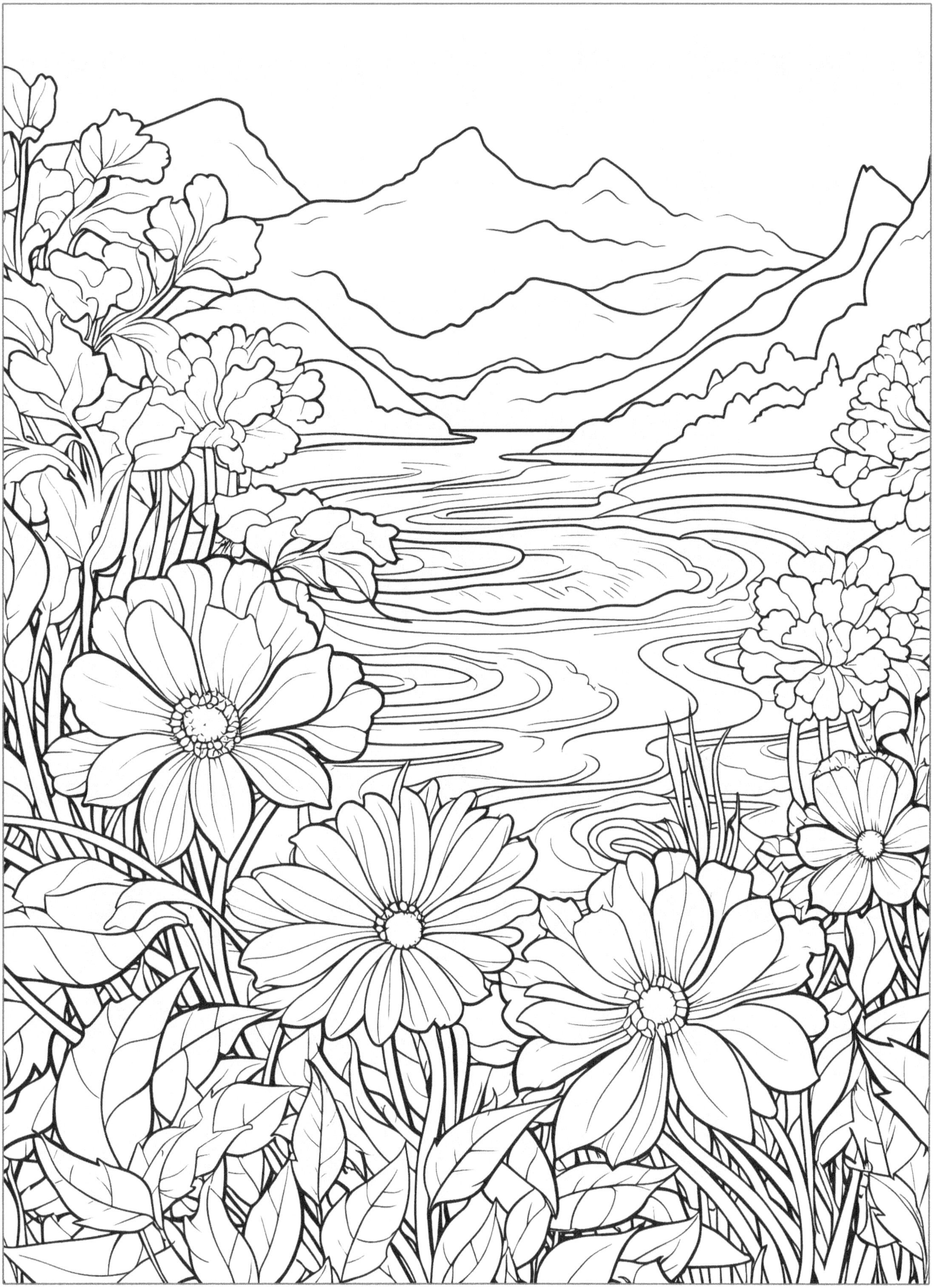

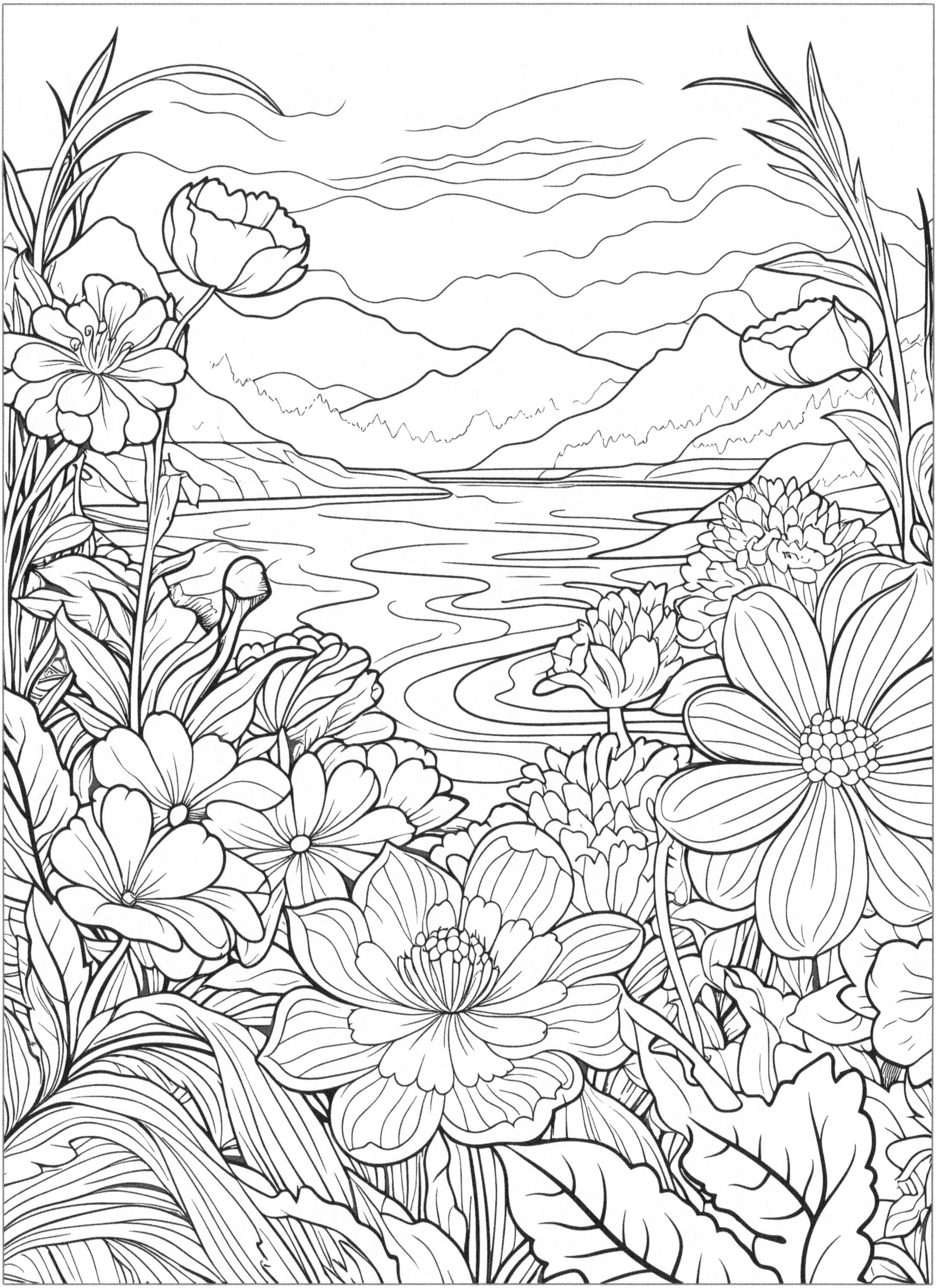

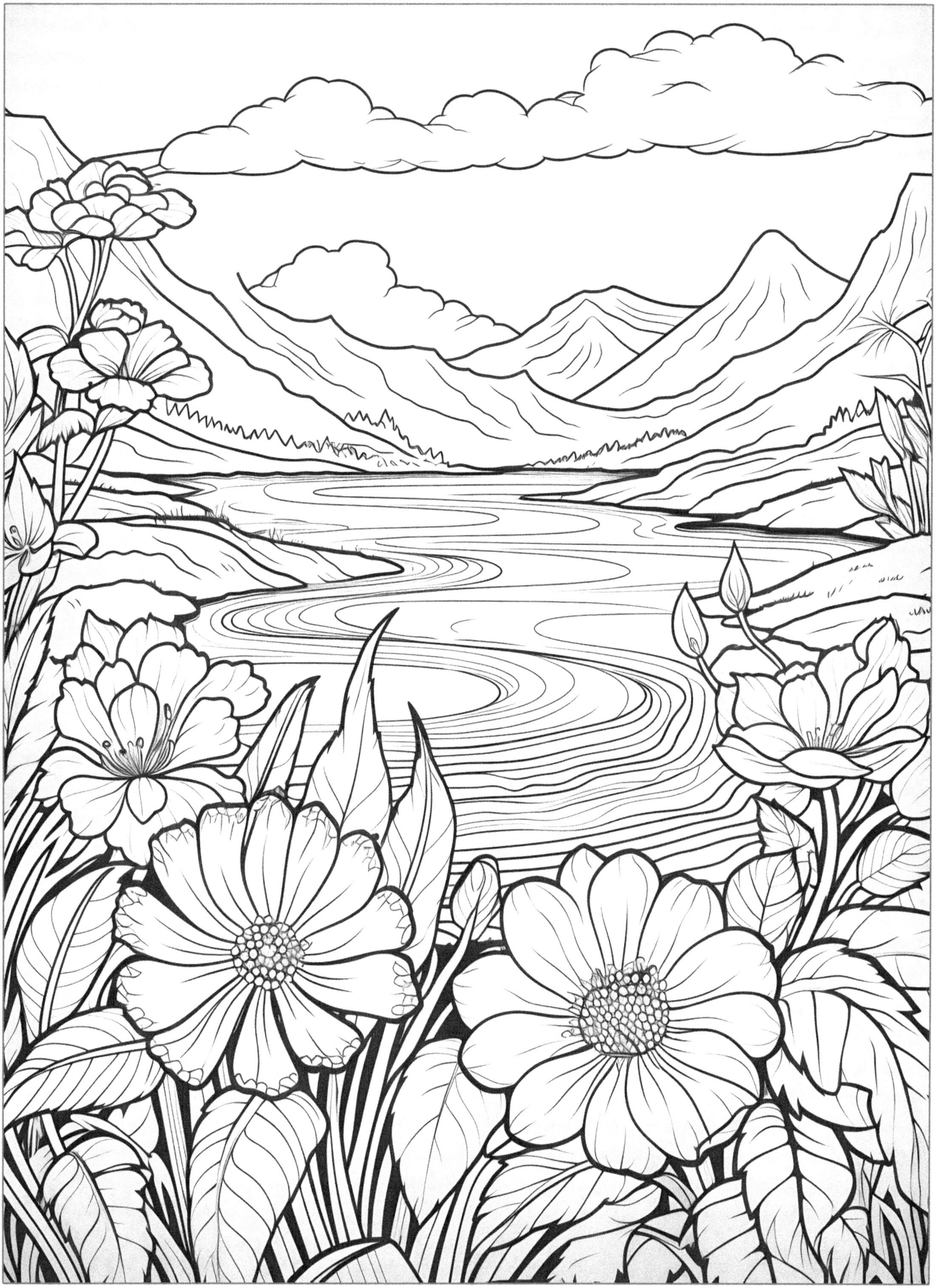

www.ingramcontent.com/pod-product-compliance
Lightning Source LLC
Chambersburg PA
CBHW082219290526
45794CB00009B/3606
* 9 7 9 8 8 7 2 8 3 0 0 8 5 *